# FRIDAYS
## WITH
# GOODMAN

A ~~Struggling~~ *STRIVING* Artist, a Good-man and
the Universal Principles at Play

WRITTEN BY MARTIN CASADO
WITH DR. LARRY GOODMAN

**Cover and Designs in the book :** Martin Casado
**Edited by:** Pat Morrissey/Havlin
**Written by:** Martin Casado
**Narrated Interviews for book with:** Dr. Larry Goodman
**Author Illustration on pages:** Martin Casado

**Title:** Fridays with Goodman- A Striving Artist, a Good-man and the Universal Principles at Play

# DEDICATIONS

To my father and mother for unintentionally guiding
me through all your ups and downs in my upbringing to
prepare me for who I am today. Ashley for being a heaven
sent and supporting me through this. Of course, Larry
Goodman for being my mentor and amazing friend, much
love to you Goodman.

# DEDICATIONS

To my wife Sally, my daughter Alexa. All of my teachers and
mentors past, present and future. And especially Martin
for recognizing there was a book here even before I did and
for putting out all of the work to make it so. And to Pat for
making what we said and wrote be readable.

# Update...

*LOADING...*

# DOWNLOAD OUR FREE ASSESMENT WHEEL BEFORE YOUR DIVE INTO FRIDAYS WITH GOODMAN AS A GIFT TO YOU!

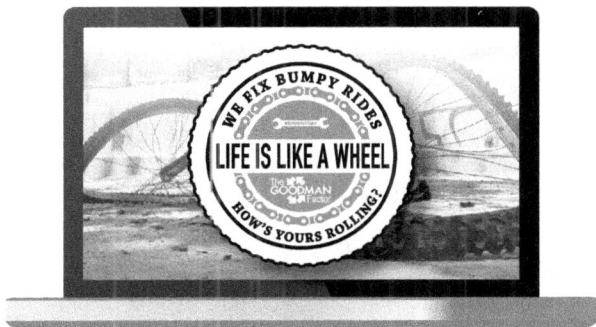

To say thank you AGAIN. We've created this tool to allow you to visually determine how your life is rolling and why? We would like to give you the wheel for FREE.

Even if you're thinking you know why your life sucks we've create this tool to help you gain awareness and perspective. We have found that people who do this before they read the book get the best results!

## DON'T WAIT!

**Watch a FREE VIDEO TRAINING ON HOW TO USE THE WHEEL now, and get your Free PDF DOWNLOAD of your WHEEL today:**

www.goodmanfactor.com/lifeislikeawheel

# CONTENTS

# INTRODUCTION

A volleyball game. A blue-eyed blonde American girl who came for the first and last time to play volleyball at the courts I played during the week needed a logo.

I am a graphic designer. It was October of 2013 when I declared a life of independence from a successful, family-run exporting company. Through a series of events that transpired during the year after my declaration to "follow my bliss," the Universe had some big lessons to teach me. I'll get back to the blonde volleyball logo encounter soon.

I was sitting on a colorful floral cushion on a wooden chair in a small room that looked like anyone's guest room. A single daybed was behind me, covered with a floral spread. A big, dark brown wooden armoire/desk is to my right, a hip-high book-shelf with the entire series of books by Steven King on my left, and a mirrored sliding door closet that showed my reflection.

On what appears to be a comfortable, tan, faux leather arm-chair sat Dr. Larry Goodman. He looked up at me while he scribbled my name and pertinent information on the form on his clipboard and said, "So what's on your mind?"

I was a little taken aback, since I had no idea of what he was offering me in exchange for my marketing services. So I told him that I read a lot, and that one of my favorite authors was Joseph Campbell. I told him my motivation for making this journey was to "follow my bliss" as Campbell says. Without missing a beat, Larry brought me crashing down to earth by saying, "It's okay to follow your bliss, just don't quit your day job." The Goodman Factor had begun.

It's funny how life works, right? No one shows you the way. You get advice, or you look up to certain people, but sometimes we need a software update. I've heard we have to unlearn to re-learn. As I look back in my life, guidance from parents, books, movies, Winnie the Pooh, successful business owners and even the bad apples of the bunch, all in the grand scheme served to make a particular impact on me at that moment in space and time to learn and grow.

In some divine order, these guides show you an interpre-tation of their lives, and, if you're willing to listen, lessons are being given. I'm not saying they are all noble, but some way, somehow, they serve a higher purpose. Along the way, knowl-edge is always being shared by people who have lived way many years before us, and yet we stubbornly know better and decline the guidance and choose to learn the hard way. Only then, in my own experience, we fail miserably and egotistically mutter,

"Yeah, yeah okay. I get it. I'll listen. I'll learn."

I remember growing up working at my father's company. My dad would always reference life's lessons with a quote or use a metaphor on what he learned along the way in his own life. That drove me crazy growing up! The funny part is, in my early 30s and even more so with the help of social media, I've become a motivational junkie, and it's become a trend that's here for the long run. I've collected quotes for years now, saving them in a file on my laptop called "Daily Motivation." I often go back to them and also have them rotate as my screen saver every 15 minutes. I often send them to motivate friends, or if someone is feeling down, I will show my "spiritual charm" by sharing a quote via text message or email and become that charming Buddha.

I had reached what most would call a "tipping point" in my life amongst my luxury leather office chair and my light tan-colored wood cubicle. My office was originally a utility area where the primary office computer servers were, with bulky filing cabinets along the walls behind me. My desk was located in the back corner next to where I could hear the humming of the computer server fans in full volume. On the opposite side at the end of the file cabinets was the office manager's desk. An older, heavy-set lady (kind of like your old school teacher from the '80s or '90s, you've seen the movie), she always wore baggy, colorful, animal-print polyester, long-sleeved shirts. She was always on the phone, chatting to clients in her Peruvian Spanish. Her voice sounded like Ecto-1, the Ghostbusters car from the '80s. It drove me to the brink of lunacy. Needless to say, I wore my headphones a lot while I worked in that confined labyrinth every day. Surrounded by my cozy dual-screen monitors, a couple photos of good times pinned to the wall and my mixture of never-returned pens (and my personal favorite blue ball-point uni-ball pens) in their spiral, designer pen holder, I knocked out my morning emails while I sipped upon my Venti® cup of black coffee with no milk or sugar, and I counted the days.

I counted the days working in my father's company because every day felt like Groundhog Day, the movie with Bill Murray. Day in and day out the only thing that changed was my CrossFit workout on the dry-erase board. I honestly felt like the official door opener and closer of my father's business because life had brought him to trust no one. My father was a hardworking man who came here from Chile with $300 in his pocket and built a very profitable business. And believe me, there was not a day growing up that he didn't tell us that story. Unfortunately, not all of us on this planet are meant to teach and, in my father's case, all he knew was that he had to be Superman.

It was my second attempt going back to dad's company. The first time I had quit at 28 years old to get a bachelor's degree in graphic design. Later, I worked for an ad agency, leaving to run my own graphic design company. Then my father's prodigy left and started his own competing company. So when your father builds a successful company and makes a great life for his family, you naturally get prepped to take the reins. It's in your cards, or so I believed, to just take this silver platter and "You'll be fine." I call it the "mafia effect" because of the loyalty side of it and because I felt like it was my duty to step up as the first-born son to fulfill my father's ultimate dream of passing along what he built from scratch. But that was just it: it was his dream, not mine.

What led me to make such a big decision to resign from my family company a second time to live my own dream? I don't really know. I often wonder if I manifested my destiny due to what I read and a burning, intuitive desire that encouraged me to trust my process. All the self-improvement books have different themes but tell the same story: someone goes out on a limb to risk it all, goes broke and later fulfills their life's purpose and writes their story. So from a series of countless audio books, physical books, premonitions, spiritual amateur enlightenments, intuitions, kiteboarding, ayahuasca, hallelujahs, Kundalini yoga and so many clueless (at the time) declarations, I decided to start my hero's journey and follow my bliss.

I am forever grateful for the quickening of events that followed. Trust me when I tell you I'm still a work in progress. I declared on that fateful October day of 2013 that I was going to begin to live my way. Or so I thought....

# CHAPTER ONE

# The Call to Encounter

*I really believe that coincidence is God's way of remaining anonymous.*

**Bill Moyers**

It was an early Friday morning, February 20, 2015, and I heard a knock on my door. It was my first meeting of the morning with a potential client who needed a website. I open the door, and there stood an older gentleman and another client and friend of mine, Angela. I held the door open and let them in to my dining room area that I had converted into my office. My desk was against the wall with two computer monitors and my office chair. Two bar stools that I also use in the kitchen area were ready to sit on. I introduced myself graciously, held out my hand and said, "Hello, pleased to meet you. My name is Martin." He said, "Hello Martin, my name is Larry."

He stood about my height, around 5'11", older, experienced, former neighborhood chiropractor with glasses, a slight gap in his front teeth, and his jacket wrapped around his right arm. I leaned over and gave a kiss on the cheek to Angela and said, "Hello Madame." It's a common greeting in most parts of Miami and how I grew up with my Hispanic parents in regard to kissing on the cheek. I had met Angela, a slender, blue-eyed, curly haired blonde, cute girl in her late 30s playing volleyball one night. We had exchanged numbers because she needed to redo her logo for a company she called "Succeed with Grace."

Before Larry sat down, he placed his jacket on my couch, then sat beside Angela on a stool chair, right next to me. We start going over the existing websites Larry shared with other doctors in his Wellness. PSI company and some other collaborations with other clients' websites. Larry is what you call an ABC'er – always be closing.* As I browsed through these websites, I began to share some random knowledge and business terms from books I had been reading over the years. I guess I was nervous and wanted to establish some kind of intellectual connection with Larry, so I blabbered away.

I chatted about some Stoicism and Taoism books I had read and the online course I was doing at the time called *The 67 Steps by Tai Lopez[1]* . You've probably seen Tai's YouTube interruptions right before you want to verify a conspiracy or view a cute dog or cat video. Surprisingly, Tai was very influential in my process and had inspired me to look for mentors and the importance of a role model in one of the videos he posted. Before The 67 Steps, I was inspired by TED Talks too. He had me with the title of his TEDx called Why I read a book a day (and why you should too): the law of 33%. Look online for it. It's why I used my last credit card credit to get The 67 Steps. It was also right before Tai saturated the market with online commercials in his large homes and garage full of cars in LA. So here I was, and I didn't know it the time, sitting next to my mentor. As Larry was to put it later, "If I were to plagiarize from Tony

---

1 Learn more about Tai Lopez and The 57 Steps go to https://www.tailopez.com/

Robbins, he has an event that he calls the Date with Destiny."

You have to understand at this time in my life I was officially broke, living a lifestyle I couldn't afford after many events leading up to this "date with destiny." I had been living a declared "creative detachment" from my family's company that I had worked for most of my life on and off, and I will get more into that later. I left that life in October of 2013 to start working full time in my own graphic design company. I was the sole proprietor who did everything. Later the Universe would show me the consequences of that. A harsh realization of my comfy life of creative work ethic and the promised declaration of following my bliss all came to harsh reality after reading one email. It was actually two emails and the Universe's unique way of lighting a fire under my ass. I was depleted and honestly lost.

First, the IRS took out around $3,500 straight from my account, where I only had about half of that amount. I received over-charge fees and a maintenance fee on top of that. The second email was from my "bread and butter" client who paid most of my bills. The proposed reduction in work dropped my monthly income by about 90% from $4-5,000 a month to $900 to eventually zero. I was in panic mode.

So, as I sit next to Larry and Angela assessing what he needs for his website and potential work we can collaborate on, Larry is giving little mini-lectures on life. Next thing you know I'm ranting to him about having gone back to get a degree in graphic design late in my 20s and now I have this huge student loan, and I have to pay this hefty fee monthly and so forth. He stops me mid-sentence and says, "You made that decision. No one other than you told you to make that choice. You went and got the student loan." He pointed his finger toward my heart, making me well aware of the accountability for my own decisions. He went on to say, "We're living in a time where we have to reassess values."

Now, under the heading of "There's nothing wasted in God's economy," meaning there are no mistakes, Larry continued, "Had you not taken out these loans, had you not been given what we're going to call the 'gift of desperation,' you and I might have never met. When you deny somebody the opportunity to experience the effect of their choices, called 'consequences,' you actually deny them the opportunity to grow and to evolve. That's the message that is being lost on at least half the newer generations. There are no victims, there are only volunteers."

That was just the point of where I was in my life, and Larry is sitting there knowing I was totally playing the violin and in full-on victim mode with myself. He looked at Angela and told her they had to show me the YouTube video titled *Bob Newhart-STOP IT*[2]. So we watch this skit from Comedy Central's MADtv. The gist of it is that a lady has a fear of being buried alive in a box. After a satirical build-up Bob has two words of wisdom. He yells "Stop it!" Larry just loses it because in what he does he sees this all the time. He would often tell me, "Most of us are addicted to our own suffering."

After the video and some general notes taken on what Larry needed for his website. We started to end the meeting. As I stood up Larry asked me to get a pen and paper. He wanted

2 To check out STOP IT go to www.goodmanfactor.com/motivationvids or https://bit.ly/1QyAtoD

me to write these seven words that he called the "seven areas of life." He put his hand on my shoulder and said, "Write this down; spiritual, mental, physical, financial, career, family and social. We'll discuss more at a later date." It was as if he knew (and he did) what was to come. We said our goodbyes, and I escorted Larry and Angela to the door. A couple of minutes later Angela calls to tell me that Larry had left his jacket and was coming back up to get it.

Later on while we were collaborating on this book, Larry said, "I've come to trust the divine order, and so when I left my jacket I knew that we were supposed to meet again. I knew that we would be meeting again as the car pulled away and I remembered my jacket. In fact, I could be wrong about this, I don't remember who said it or where, or maybe it's just a tactic that I've heard that, umm, how can I put this tactfully. Women who can potentially turn into overnight visitors on occasion will leave something behind as a societally acceptable reason to have to reconnect in case the man doesn't call the next day." I humorously respond, "I was going to call you, Larry, I was gonna call you back, baby." We laugh, and he tells me, "But do you get my point, Casanova?" I sure did understand that story all too well, and in my gift of desperation I had left the belly of the whale and entered onto the road of trials.

## Universal Insight:

*You market the illusion to the many and
the few will see the truth.*

# CHAPTER TWO

# The Factors of "The Good Man"

*The only impossible journey is the one you never begin.*

**Anthony Robbins**

---

Hi Larry, 2/26/15

I received your email and it was great meeting you! How did the other meeting go?

I would really like to get some coffee or get together sometime and talk if you don't mind. You're like everything I've read and so beyond it makes a sort of comfort come alive in me. Like I'm on the right path. You let me know.

Thank you!!

Martin Casado

---

Yes, I wrote that above email just like that. Could I have edited it and doctored up my wording. Maybe, but I didn't. Right now as I write this chapter, I see in my document that little green squiggly grammatical error in my Word document was telling me to take off the "s" in "makes" but I won't. Then, I won't be authentic, and that specifically is how I felt when I met Larry. It's like Rick Sapio said, in an entrepreneur course I went to in Dallas, Texas with Larry as well. Rick said, "When you find that perfect CEO to run your company after so many interviews, you just want to get up and hug him in the final interview before hiring him!" Larry would tell me, "So in a world that's thriving for authenticity, now the answer really is 'Stop it.' Don't pretend to make up a reason to stay in communication with someone. If you want to remain in communication with someone, remain in contact with that somebody."

In many readings, a common theme starts to appear, and you start to see the pattern of coincidences being a domino effect set in motion. The seasons in your life are in full effect, the good with the bad. Life's coincidences are in no way coincidences. With that being said, to meet Larry at this moment in my life was the Universe's way of being anonymous.

Before I met Larry in early 2015, in order to encounter or meet him, you would have to know what he does or the regular times he goes to Starbucks for iced coffee and the morning paper. Larry said, "You'd have to call me a boutique, under the radar, referral-only consulting company." He explained, "If a client got referred to me, and in retrospect I guess it would be called an arrogant pride, if he found me he was supposed to. I am about as hard a person to find because I don't have a website, I don't have my phone listed, there's no sign on the door, and I don't promote anything. It's all word of mouth, and so if you wind up in my chair you just are supposed to be there." He continued, "Now, talk about coincidences. So the guy referred to me, who happened to be a web developer, tells me, 'Listen, you already helped me immeasurably and I have to tell you this: You have no right to keep what it is you do a secret. There are too many people that need this.' And I said 'Hmmm.'"

I asked Larry where his company name, The Goodman Factor, came from. "That name was given to me by a client of mine as he was referring another client. He called me up and said he had someone who needed to see me. He needed The Goodman Factor. I said, 'What do you mean, The Goodman factor. What's that?' My friend says, 'Well, you know that thing that happens to people when they stop listening to the BS they were brought up with and start listening to what you put there?'" Larry remembers sitting there and going, "That's it. That really is it."

I asked him what got him to where he was. He said, "I'm always looking to up my game. Always seeking to add value to an ongoing application of teachers and mentors in virtual time and on to full access because my time with Dr. John Demartini, whom I've been mentored by since 1992, is limited by space and time with the fact that he's traveling all over the place. Now with the Business Finishing School, I now have a virtual presence that lets me study wherever I am."

I had gone earlier that year with Larry to Dallas, Texas to a Business Mastery Bootcamp[3], a three-day event on exponential business growth and success, an intense weekend of hearing two amazing entrepreneurs, Rick Sapio and Dr. Patrick Gentempo, share their real-life successes and failures. I didn't know it at that time but Larry was prepping me to understand the principles and disciplines to run a successful company. If I applied the Business Finishing School applications and modules properly, I technically could be running multiple companies globally.

---

3 Check out the Business-Mastery Bootcamp at https://businessfinishingschool.com/

Twice that year I attended the Business Finishing School, the second time alone because Larry had a speaking engagement in Orlando. I had redesigned the covers for the workbooks for the next boot camp, and although they didn't end up using them due to the timing of the books going to print, my boot camp attendance was comped. I even got a shout-out from Rick Sapio congratulating me on the creativity of the covers.

"So, maximum evolution occurs at the border of support and challenge, that's the universal law," says Larry. "In case you haven't noticed, we're living in it right now. When there's a period of rapid change, people wake up with the sense of 'I don't know what's happening but there's something different, and I don't know what to do.' When people don't know what to do, the only thing they know is what they used to do. The solution, the general consensus, I hear is, 'I'll just do what I used to do only I'll do it more, I'll do it louder, I'll do it differently, I'll do it bigger but don't tell me I have to change what I do. Because what I do is so intimately connected to who I am, if I had to change what I do I'd be lost.' In fact, when you do NET (Neuro Emotional Technique) with these people, that's the emotion that comes up: They're lost.

"So we're literally in between a distinction between human-doing instead of human-being and we've lost our humanity."

## Universal Insight:

*The Universe doesn't give you more than you can handle.*

# CHAPTER THREE
## My Lucky Break

*Just let go. Let go of how you thought your life*
*should be, and embrace the life that is trying to*
*work its way into your consciousness.*

**Caroline Myss**

The more I learn about my own journey, I assess my own awareness of being careful what you ask for because you might just get it. In my family company I worked with my sister, and when I announced my resignation was coming soon she asked me, "Why are you doing this now? Dad's not the easiest to work with, but you have it all here." I told her, "Pam, please trust in your brother. I have to do this."

"What's so bad about being the neighborhood chiropractor," Larry says as he has in many different times to me in our sessions. "There were a bunch of people around me who would say, 'Look how many people you help. Look how much money you make. Look at the great life you live.'" Then with some aggravation, Larry raises his voice and says, "And meanwhile inside I'm going, 'Faaaaaaaaaaaack. I don't want to do this. It's killing me!'

"So the Universe says, 'Okay, buddy... no worries... you're never doing it again!'"

"Now I take it you're going to tell me how you got your lucky break," I say in a satirical way. Larry's not sure this story should go in this book, but he begins. First, he tells me that when he was young, he used to go roller skating. "The roller skates had four wheels and the breaks were in the front," he remembers. "So, I was supposed to take my daughter roller blading, and I go to pick her up, and it's a Sunday, and I don't even remember what I said or did that my former wife went bat-shit crazy and told me I was not going. So I left and was more than a little pissed off. One of the things I found out later was the incidence of injury doing high-risk activity when you are emotionally upset is 7 to 15 times the normal. Now I know when you feel stressed out and you want to blow off some steam, go do something, but you'd better make it something that doesn't involve a lot of risks. So it's 5 p.m. in the afternoon and I'm still furious, so I'm going to blow off some steam and go roller blading. I'm in front of the Coral Gables Youth Center. There's a curb at the end of the sidewalk, and I know I need to stop and I had a brain fart. Instead of putting my heel down like I know I'm supposed to, I put my toe down and the instant I put my toe down I know I'm f---ed. I go off the edge of the curb and fall back into the curb. The curb has now become a wedgie. I break the femur clean off the neck – it breaks in 3 pieces – and I bounce. On the bounce, I blow out my linear lateral meniscus. When I come to rest, I cannot move."

Larry continues, "When I finally get to the hospital, and they've looked at the thing, I find out it's the most potentially fatal fracture of the long bone. The jagged edge of my femur has come within a millimeter of piercing my colon or nicking the femoral artery. The orthopedic surgeon, who has since become one of my good friends, puts me back together. All I want to know is when I can run again. He says, 'No, you're done. You're done. You'll never normally walk or run again. You'll probably never practice again.' I was in utter disbelief."

So Larry went through three surgeries and two and half years of PT rehab. It gives him the time to access who he was. He continues, "And what am I doing because – and listen to the metaphor – I can't run away from it. I can't move away from it. All there is is me and the chair. That's when the logo Wellness PSI began, the beginning to make the transition from hands-on chiropractic to something else. That's when the whole thing happened.

"Divine intervention – there's nothing wasted in God's economy, its divine design," Larry says. "I was a very impatient guy. I know consciously I would have said, "WHAT THE F--K, I CAN'T! Again, I was much too impatient, I needed results, and I needed them now! Three surgeries and two and half years of PT. I was out of my mind!"

I recall that I remember a protégé to my father, who he was hoping would take over the company, left after many years and started his own business that would compete against my father. Needless to say, my father reached out to me and proposed a deal I couldn't resist, basically matching what I was making at the time. Out of loyalty and for the love of my family, I went back, leaving my graphic design company.

I was older then, and I was helping other companies build their brands. I can do this, I told myself, and my father has changed, I wishfully thought. Not even a year back, I was getting a haircut and the guy steps back and asks, "Homie, did you cut yourself or shave a circle in the back of your head?" He showed me that I literally had a bald spot the size of a quarter on the back of my head. I was in shock. There was literally no hair there. Funny enough, a year before that when my brother worked for my father, he had the same quarter-sized bald spot in the exact area where mine was. We both no longer work in the family biz. By the way, this is just one of many tipping points that lead me to my journey in knowing there is more to life than what is set in stone in front of me.

"Yup, now when I said it wouldn't go away," Larry says, "There was so much residual demand chiropractically, I didn't know how to say no. So, I wound up doing coaching, some chiropractic, booking a gig here and there. I didn't know how to promote coaching – it really only happens by accident. So I did what human nature would do. You go with what you know. You know what I'm saying?" Larry asks with almost a shrug.

## The 4 Levels of Knowingness:

When you know something intellectually but you're not living it, that's one level. The next level knows that you know it, meaning you preach with a level of awareness. The third level knows that you know that you know it, which is where it starts showing up in your actions. The fourth, which is really the deepest one, is, "When you know that you know that you know that you know it." Where anything that doesn't align with that truth that becomes what you start to notice and it stands out like a sore thumb, and then you get to look and see why you're resisting what you know to be the truth[4].

## Universal Insight:

*You're always exactly where you're supposed to be, doing what you're exactly supposed to be doing — trust your process.*

---

4 Download a Free Meme on the 4 levels of Knowingness at
www.fridayswithgoodman.com/bookbonusmaterial

# CHAPTER FOUR

# It's Okay to Ask for Help

*The truth is that our finest moments are most likely to occur when we are feeling deeply uncomfortable, unhappy, or unfulfilled. For it is only in such moments, propelled by our discomfort, that we are likely to step out of our ruts and start searching for different ways or truer answers.*

**Penney Peirce**


After about a year into my second attempt in my mid-30s at leaving the family business and my declared independence, I finally moved into my own place alone. I resigned on the first of October 2013, the same day my lease was up on my high-rise in a posh area in the Brickell area of Miami where I had a roommate. I also booked a month's trip to Europe and decided to pick a place to live when I got back. I figured I could sleep on people's couches or crash with my father until I found a place. I was living in the moment and "just following my bliss," but I had only read about this power and clearly had no idea what I was doing.

I was living off two graphic design clients, one who paid me very well and another on a monthly retainer. This gave me the confidence to go out on my own, run my design company and finally live on my own. I was your in-house/out-house designer ready at your disposal, a sole proprietor. I had no real structured discipline. I mean, I was always responsible for my deadlines and did quality, detailed work but juggling the administrative – handling my taxes, proposals, the deadlines, the creativity, the phone calls and accounts receivables – was all done by the seat of my pants. I kept pushing aside responsibility and inventing every excuse not to deal with the nitty-gritty tedious details required to run a business. I wasn't running my business at all like a business. In the words of Larry, "The purpose of business is to have a living laboratory within which to live and breathe laws of the Universe in saying, 'I'm open for business.'" I wasn't doing any of this, and it led me into a downward spiral and, man, the Universe had lessons for me!

One big lesson is having all your eggs in one basket and losing them all in one email. Your big money clients say sorry, we're restructuring and are only going to need a few things from you from now on. All the stages of grief come into your life: denial with excuses, anger, victim mode, negotiations with yourself and blame, depression consisting of lots of sleep, not wanting to get out of bed and, lastly, acceptance of your own mediocrity.

Even in my social life, as I look back now, I wasn't that great of a person. I barely kept a relationship beyond a month, and even then I was juggling many women at a time. It was so addicting. I remember by Wednesdays I had already started texting cute, humorous little messages to get the weeknights and weekend planned out. It was exhausting and what was I trying to prove? Drinking on the weekends heavily, FOMO (fear of missing out), over-spending on things I couldn't afford, pleasing various groups of friends I had. Filling the void, scared of commitment, excuse after excuse – all in all I was avoiding not allowing myself to take responsibility and grow the f--k up already.

Now, I come from a good upbringing materialistically, with family issues and divorced parents who were together for 28 years. Overall I've had an amazing life in hindsight, and I complain based upon the level of my upbringing mindset. Meaning I was raised in this lifestyle, and it was all I knew. In declaring your independence from a family business and following your own entrepreneurial spirit is not easy. Seeking help sometimes is not easy either. Facing your failures and understanding that we're never alone in this process and asking for help is okay. In fact, it's an enormous liberation if you set your ego aside. I always said I should get help and see a psychiatrist. Yet, like my business, I put that off too. I'll do it as soon as I start bringing in enough income, I always said.

"Fear is an assumption that you're about to experience in the future," Dr. Demartini said in one of his talks on fear. I felt the fear. I also knew that with struggle and failures came opportunity and experience. At least that's what all the books, seminars and YouTubes I've read and listened to were always preaching. I had all these tools and tactics, but I lacked my values, discipline and, most importantly, my true authenticity. I just didn't know how to properly use them, and I needed a new update to my subconscious software. I needed to find my inner good-man.

## Universal Insight:

*When the student is ready, the teacher will appear.*

## CHAPTER FIVE

# The Arrangement

*Desire is the starting point of all achievement, not a hope, not a wish, but a keen pulsating desire which transcends everything.*

**Napoleon Hill**

It's funny the way the Universe works because I really had no clue what Larry was offering me in exchange for taking care of his marketing. Angela, who had introduced us and brought him to my apartment, really didn't tell me much other than some process he did called NET and that he did coaching. I honestly thought he was still a chiropractor of some sort; I really had no clue. We went back and forth on emails and text messages to find a time that we could stay on schedule every week to meet. Being a graphic designer and working late hours I wanted to change my sleeping patterns and wake up earlier. So, I picked an early Friday morning at 9 a.m.

When I asked him how he met Angela. Larry answered, "I'm always seeking tools by which to unravel and uncover people's inner potential. So someone suggested that I go to a PSYCH-K® course because it was a similar method of communicating with the unconscious like NET, and that's where I met Angela." Was he doing PSYCH-K before NET? He says with a subtle laugh, "Oh yeah, 20 years before." PSYCH-K stands for psychological kinesiology[5], a set of principles and processes designed to change subconscious beliefs that limit the expression of your full potential as a spiritual being having a human experience. Angela explained a little to me about some aspects of psychological kinesiology in shifts in consciousness, and she was very passionate about it. Larry would reference some details from it in our sit-downs. The Goodman Factor was coming together.

Now, what is NET? Larry tells me it stands for Neuro Emotional Technique. The website www.netmindbody.com says, "NET is a mind-body technique that uses a methodology of finding and removing neurological imbalances related to the physiology of unresolved stress. NET is a tool that can help improve many behavioral and physical conditions."

Larry explains, "When NET first started, H.U.Y.A. stood for Hold-Up-Your-Arm because that's how the testing begins. It became like the secret handshake among people who were doing NET. The greeting became 'Huyaaa!' like the Marines, you know. In NET language, the way the dialogue gets started between the client and the practitioner is to find out what you are not okay with that you'd like to be. Or what do you think you're okay with, but you're not sure. And that becomes the first reason that the client holds their arm up."

I asked Larry why, when we first started together, we didn't do the arm up, the NET process for a while. "Because I don't just have only NET in my toolbox, you see. So, I'm looking at things like your body posture, pupillary blink rate, fluctuations of the carotid artery pulse and, um, it would take a very long time to go through the whole list of the stuff that I'm subtly and

5 To learn more about Psych-K, go to https://www.psych-k.com.

not so subtly monitoring as we have a conversation," he says.

We were exchanging services where I would create the brand for The Goodman Factor and eventually do the website. I completed a number of logo choices. To pick that final one Larry took the various choices to a Dr. John Demartini conference he was attending. Within the group members and Demartini, he narrowed it down to the current one we use. I thought that was pretty impressive, a great compliment.

Later, as we continued meeting on our Friday mornings and I was coming into my own, internally connecting to my inner good-man, I almost felt a sense of irresponsibility because I felt like I owed him more. My subconscious was recalibrating. I was identifying blocks in my life and confronting them, learning to take full responsibility for my actions, and understanding I'm not alone in all of this. I tell Larry that I know the hourly rate he charges his clients to sit in this chair to see him. On top of that, he had a waiting list. At that point in my life, there was no way I could afford him.

"My understanding of our respective roles in each other's lives is, 'It is what it is,'" he said. "We're like co-creating this thing and so, let me put it this way, it's clear to me beyond a shadow of a doubt that your role of this, especially in our whole process of The Goodman Factor – until you came along the marketing didn't get done. So I both honor and respect your sense on how you want creatively for this to go."

## Universal Insight:

*The Universe rewards persistence and perseverance.*

# CHAPTER SIX

# Frames in a Movie

*To perceive the world differently, we must be
willing to change our belief system, let the past
slip away, expand our sense of now, and dissolve
the fear in our minds*

**William James**

Let me explain a little bit of our process when I'm sitting with Larry in our sessions. We usually start off with light conversation about current events, a little bit about things on my mind. He reaches down and grabs his pad, and somewhere in between his dialogue and mine, we touch upon a sensitive subject, an "NEC."

Larry says, "So when you take a look at the people in your life, instead of viewing them as people, you look at them as snapshots. Here is the connection to NET. If, instead of seeing them as snapshots, you know them as frames in a movie, then you wouldn't be attached to that snapshot. Before there were video tapes and DVDs, they had this stuff called movie film. You ever see it? The individual frames are parts of the whole movie when they're in a flow. Now what happens sometimes is when there's too much emotional charge on one individual frame, you get stuck there. That's what they call in NET practice a Neural Emotional Complex (NEC), and that becomes a problem."

He explains, "So, I introduce one of my clients to NET. We cleared an NEC that had to do with her mother. When she was 17 she watched her mother, who was the strongest person she ever knew in her life, have a nervous breakdown. She thought her mother was going to fall apart and, therefore, that she would have to fall apart too. An NEC (Neural Emotional Complex) is the picture I was talking about, the snapshot. In that client's case, it was the snapshot of her mother falling apart. That's the sensitizing event. That's the point in space-time that you get experientially locked in, where you forget that the game is rigged and you can't fail. You forget everything is going to be fine."

There's a certain beautiful feeling about knowing that, I tell Larry, understanding it's all an illusion, and it's all rigged in our favor with proper values, discipline and faith in the process. "Well, yes," he replies, "remember I said to you a master is someone who found out. So once you've been to one side of the hill, and now you're climbing the hill when you get to look down the hill and recognize that you've been there. There's a certain amount of comfort and ease. Certainly that's the path that you're on, and the guides that you're following will get you wherever it is you need to be.

"When you under-promise and over-deliver and you enable people to see a part of themselves that's more or better or different than what they ever thought they had, the only thing left to say is thank you," Larry says. "And in the face of that thank you, you get to raise your prices." We both start laughing and I'm laughing right now at 2:58 a.m. as I'm writing this.

He continues, "Because it's how you get to be aware, that it's not about the intrinsic value, it's about the extrinsic value. Extrinsic motivation refers to behavior that is driven by external rewards such as money, fame, grades and praise. Intrinsic motivation refers to behavior that is driven by internal rewards, in other words, motivation to engage in a behavior because you enjoy it or find it interesting. This will occur when we act without any obvious external rewards. We simply enjoy an activity or see it as an opportunity to explore, learn and actualize our potential.

"One of my clients takes boudoir photos of her clients and has them connect with their innermost beauty," Larry says. "And what's that worth? If you can give someone a picture that makes them see themselves as more beautiful than they ever thought they were – that's priceless!"

## Universal Insight:

*I have no clue what's in my best interest.*

# CHAPTER SEVEN

# One Foot on the Gas,
# the Other Foot on the Brake

*There is nothing so wretched or foolish as to anticipate misfortunes. What madness it is in your expecting evil before it arrives!*

**Seneca**

"What is this whole knee-to-knee process?" I ask Larry. "Why, when I sit with you in our sessions, are our knees are so close together we're practically playing patty cake?"

"That was a combination of my work in NET and my work with Demartini. The purpose of the knee-to-knee is to close the circle of energy very tight so that, if you pardon the expression, there's nowhere to hide. And also to create the space base in which to the unconscious gets to come up and say, 'Okay (with a long pause), is it safe for me to come out and sort through this stuff?' Which is where, if you remember during my first session, is 'What happens in these four walls stays within these four walls.' And I'm like the priest, and there's no judgment,"

Larry chuckles and continues. "All of that is the psychic informed consent.

"Then there's the fact that it's knee-to-knee and there's an opportunity for the two energy spheres to interact, that whole personal space thing. You understand I set it up to start that way so that there's the possibility to trigger the personal space thing. Now I've never tracked the percentage, but what I'll tell you is the more damaged the new client is the further they pull the chair away. Which then gives me feedback about how quickly I can progress with them, how defended and guarded they are. The next thing is that there are mirrored closet doors in my room because some people can't look at themselves. They just don't even want to look at those mirrors. And they will turn the chair away from the mirror," Larry says.

Yes, I tell Larry, I have had some of those days in our sessions, and I've scooted back a little to pan out from the mirror.

"The questionnaire is only three pages long but you'd be surprised to see that some people don't get past the first page," Larry continues describing his process. "My instruction is always 'Let me know when you're finished. There's a questionnaire on the clipboard.' I'll wait and give them time to be with themselves and the questionnaire. I might pop my head in and say, 'Do you have any questions?'"

I asked Larry if there was more to this whole set up, and he says he has a separate questionnaire for a person who was coming in for more body-related issues. Next I ask what was his signature introduction when taking a new client.

He says, "What do you want? What are you not okay with that you'd like to be okay with? Or what do you think you're okay with, but you're not sure?"

In one of our sessions I tell Larry that I remember I was complaining about my clients asking for insane amounts of edits to the designs and having me work crazy hours to meet the deadline. Then later they take ridiculous amounts of time to pay me. I remember he asked me if I realized the words I was using to describe my situation. He got up from his chair and retrieved one of about a dozen rubber bands that were behind his door on the door knob. He placed it around my wrist and told me, "Every time you catch yourself saying crazy, ridiculous or any of those words, you give yourself a little snap on the wrist. Listen to the words that you are telling your conscious mind. When you say these particular words, you are going to manifest them. What's the definition of insanity? It's doing the same thing over and over and expecting a different result, right?"

Needless to say, in applying the exercise to myself, in consciously choosing better adjectives and reprogramming my negative associations to describe my day, my wrist became pretty sore, but it worked.

Larry explained, "This is the rubber band effect of people's conscious language and people's unconscious language. Individuals who are high achievers could describe their day by saying they had a crazy day. Now, the theory is they want more, but consider the conflicted drive of wanting 'more crazy.' Can you see why your life could be a roller coaster? It creates what's called an approach-avoidance, like you're driving a car with one foot on the gas and the other foot on the brake. And the creator and the Universe say, 'Dude, which one do you want?' Because you can have more or you can have crazy, but if you have more and crazy, you're going to wear out the parts. It is not sustainable."

## Universal Insight:

*The opposite of momentum is complacency. And it is important to remember: Momentum cures everything.*

# CHAPTER EIGHT

# Just Because You Can Doesn't Mean You Should

*Because one believes in oneself, one doesn't try to convince others. Because one is content with oneself, one doesn't need others' approval. Because one accepts oneself, the whole world accepts him or her.*

**Lao-Tzu**

On my drive over to see Larry on a beautiful, sunny, congested Miami causeway, I started to think that I had no comparison in going to a "shrink," as the term goes, and Larry's services. I had thought at one point in my life I should maybe see a psychologist/therapist. I had no reference in comparing our NET sessions and a psychiatrist. The NET and his business coaching was something I wanted to share with my friends and family because I was improving so quickly. I parked my car in the grass, walked up to his door and rang the doorbell. Larry answers the door and greets me with a hug. As usual his official greeter, Buddy, a Pekingese bundle of joy, awaits his loving scratch behind the ear. I place my bag down, sit in my wooden chair, and we begin.

So what's the difference between you and a psychologist? I ask Larry, wanting to know the difference since I had never been to any therapy or didn't even know what I was getting myself into.

A little thrown back, Larry says "Oh, my god" and starts laughing in his endearing manner. He says, "When going to a psychologist you don't find out anything about the psychologist because they're supposed to be the uninvolved backdrop and are not supposed to put forth their opinion. In my own experience, the premise of psychology is that you can think your way into right acting. And the premise of The Goodman Factor is that you can act your way into right thinking. Understanding is just the booby prize, the 'so what?' prize. It's the prize that you get when you miss the first prize so that you won't feel bad. Another example: Understanding why you're an asshole is the booby prize. But what's crucial is to stop being an asshole."

So I say, tongue-in-cheek to get a good reaction from Larry and he doesn't disappoint, "But what if I like being an asshole?"

He laughs, "Well, if you like being an asshole then you have to be willing to bear the consequences of your ass-ho-liness. And here are what the consequences are because it's what's happening right now with the millennials. You're going to grow up, age-wise, and still be living in your parent's house. You're going to have accumulated a mass amount of student loan debt because you didn't think it through that you were going to have to pay it back. You may wind up – oh, I don't know – fathering a bunch of illegitimate children because you didn't think that when the sperm meets the egg, you could create a living, breathing being. I mean, go down the list!"

He continues but makes the example more personal. "So listen, I don't know all the particulars on how your family business ran but having a family business that you can fall back on is a little bit like that. Therein lies the difference between self-worth and self-esteem[6]. Self-worth is the result of who you are. Self-esteem is the result of what you do. And if you don't have a sense of which you are, what winds up happening is you feel you can never do enough."

Yes, I have that feeling often, the "not enough" feeling. I tell Larry I was brought up in a privileged life in the material sense. My father came here with $300 in his pocket. He worked hard every day and built a very successful exporting company. The only problem was my dad himself is a man with a past – as I hear in various stories from older relatives – which was not a pleasant one growing up in Chile. He came to the United States at 21 years old, and he holds many NECs (neural emotional complexes) in his life. Those NECs are the cause of what you're experiencing in helping me in taking back my self-esteem, I say to Larry, and more than ever my self-worth, my authentic self.

As we work together in many of our talks inside and outside of our sessions, I see this feeling of self-worth is cross-generational and affects all social classes. From the impoverished, the middle class and the wealthy class there is an epidemic of untreated worth. In my life, my parent's self-worth reflected

---

6 Free meme on Self-Esteem vs. Self-Worth at www.goodmanfactor.com/bookbonusmaterial

in me begging for validation and until this day working like I need to do more. What I try to tell Larry is we all have the same self-esteem issues whether poor or rich or what have you.

Larry says, "Absolutely! What do they call them, trust-fund babies? I remember when I was in practice this family built a business that became a national and then an international brand of a commercial exterminating company. The dad started the company with a $5,000 loan from an uncle, and he began the business literally on the kitchen table in his house. As the company grew and ultimately became international, the toughest thing he had to deal with, and the arguments he had with his wife, had to do with instilling a work ethic and a sense of the value of money in the kids. The big lesson about anything really is: Just because you can do a thing doesn't mean you should."

That little saying, "Just because you can do a thing doesn't mean you should," changed my life, I tell Larry. I did so many things over and over under that consensus of doing things just because I knew I could.

"Well, you know what?" Larry says. "Take what you just said to me and turn it into a testimonial and put it on the website because, Martin, that's real. What you just did, that's a spontaneous utterance of the value of The Goodman Factor. It's not rehearsed, it was unprompted and it's the real deal. Now really and truly for me, as much as I like the money, what you just told me made my day because that's the real reason I do what I do. That's what's having a global impact is all about. That's how you create a legacy. Legacy in Business Finishing

School is about the financial and business legacy, but a legacy in the way Dr. John Demartini speaks of it is about having an immortal effect. And that's how you have an immortal effect, so thank you for sharing that with me. It makes my day and makes what I do worthwhile, so thank you."

## Universal Insight:

*The Law of Correspondence: This law places us in the driver's seat of our own life. Your outer world will be a direct reflection of your inner world, accepting responsibility for your life.*

# CHAPTER NINE

# Why Is This Happening to Me?

*Life is like arriving late for a movie, having to figure out what was going on without bothering everybody with a lot of questions, and then being unexpectedly called away before you find out how it ends.*

**Joseph Campbell**

I was looking over my notes from our first day together that Friday morning and there was the quote I was living defiantly by, which was "Follow your bliss" by Joseph Campbell. Larry had quickly, without missing a beat, told me, "Follow your bliss, but don't quit your day job." Those words floored me as if I was catching a glimpse of the man behind the curtain, a reference Larry says often. I had jumped into my journey of "going for it" and taking the leap of faith. Inspired by the books, audio books, YouTube mentors, social media memes like "Eagles don't fly with pigeons" or "Even legends started out as amateurs" (a good Buddha quote) or even the Persian Sufi poet Rumi's, "As you start to walk out on the way, the way appears." Larry says, "The willing to bear discomfort is the touchstone of spiritual growth."

As I read over my first page of notes I read d-e-n-i-a-l as the acronym is for Don't Even Notice I Am Lying. Larry had defined it further: "Yeah, to yourself." He explained to me the three A's of change, which are Awareness, Acceptance and Appropriate action. At that time in my life things were not going blissfully; they were blissfully falling apart in many areas in both my business and personal life. As we restructured all of those areas little by little, he told me about a mantra that he used himself.

That mantra: "Even when things don't appear to be going my way, I'm certain that the living God has something even better planned for me." (I have this mantra in my Post-it® notes on my computer to go back to during those worrisome moments in my life.)

"That's really what creative destruction is all about," Larry points out. "Creative destruction is when you aren't attached to the outcome, and you have faith and certainty that the process of evolution is always maximum evolution occurring at the border of support and challenge. So that in the course of tearing something down you allow it to reform in a way that the new improved consciousness is heightened. And you see if you know that mantra is genuine and you could live that truth, then you can practice what I call radical acceptance and non-attachment. Meaning, things are going to come and things are going to go, and that's as it should be."

Why did this happen to me? I ask, aggravated at the process in total victim mode. Larry laughs as if hearing this for the hundredth, if not thousandth, time. I continue as Larry is still in mid-laugh and complain that I did all the right things. I read more than most people. I rationalize optimistically. I meditate, do yoga and for the most part eat the proper nutrition. I work a profession that I'm good at and make money from it. Why did this happen to me?

Larry just says, "That's why."

"Why?!" I ask. He says "When the student is ready, the teacher arrives."

My ego wants a better answer than that. Isn't there a molecular level mixed with the molecules and the nucleus that hypothesize the sad story I'm living out? Playing the world's smallest violin for myself inspires an answer to my question.

Larry says, without missing a beat, "Well yeah, so you understand one meaning of the word coincidence, right? Now, literally in physics, a coincidence is when two or more particles that started their path in space-time have a point where they coincide, meaning there comes a moment where their individual paths come upon the same moment in space-time and cross. So here is an example. My friend Jim and I have known each other for 35 years; he was one of my technique instructors in chiropractic school. We moved down to Florida at almost the same time. We started out in our practices, he in north West Palm Beach and me in Coral Gables/South Miami, at almost the same time and now we're partners."

I chuckle and say, "Thirty-five years, damn." Larry laughs and says, "Yeah, don't you get it?

"Let's ask the question you just asked. Why did this happen to me, right now? Eventually you stop asking why and you just say, 'Thank you.'"

I just smiled and completely understood at that moment, and felt a sense of ease.

"Again I'll tell you, the willingness to bare discomfort is the touchstone of spiritual growth," Larry says. "So here's the other truth of it: Life is what happens to you while you were in the process of trying to make happen what you thought was supposed to happen. In other words, I didn't set out one day and say, 'Hey Jim, let's build this thing together.'"

Grasping an understanding of what Larry was explaining to me, I said, "So you said these kinds of words and declarations to the Universe and then whatever came next, good or bad, were all the effects of what you wanted in the next two to 35 years?"

"Yes," he answers. "In fact, I was talking to Jim yesterday on my three areas of awareness to change that I told you earlier – awareness, acceptance and the appropriate action – and he just started laughing. I asked him what was so funny. Jim asked where I got that and continued to explain that in one of the first books he wrote in 1980 – something dealing with the stress mechanism – those were the three components to stress that he wrote. Now, I never read the book he wrote. When you read so much or hear various mediums in life, how do you recognize where you got your enlightenment from? I got it somewhere else, and that's what he wanted to know. So the point is that there is a big Library in the sky that is the storehouse of all wisdom, and what we call knowledge and discovery are really that satori moment when you bump into something that you think is a discovery, and you turn ego-driven and say, 'Look what I found!'

"This is how you learn to trust yourself; there's nothing that's not relevant. And eventually, you'll stop asking that question: Why is this happening to me?"

## Universal Insight:

*The Universe is a perfect, self-correcting system with multiple direct and indirect feedback loops to enable us to grow and evolve as spiritual beings having a human experience.*

# CHAPTER TEN

# Are You Paying Attention?

*I have lived on the lip of insanity, wanting to
know reasons, knocking on a door. It opens.
I've been knocking from the inside.*

Rumi

"When I moved down to Florida, I wound up meeting
Herb, and Herb and I were partners, from 1980 to, I guess 88,
89 whatever," Larry says and thinks a little bit. "Hmm, I'm having my own epiphany right now." He laughs and continues, "I
attempted to duplicate that over and over and over again. I was
looking for another Herb."

"So Herb pushed and challenged you?" I ask.

"Hell, yeah! Listen to this, Martin. He was the father figure in practice I never had. Then, I became the father figure for
I don't even know how many students, clients, whatever, okay?
So, I'd been looking for someone to play with, to play the big
game. Now, the closest I've been able to come to finding that
game was my buddy Neil in Daytona, and we've done some little stuff together. But he just wasn't the one."

It's funny you bring that up, I tell Larry, because I was
working late the other night. As I work on my design projects,
as long as there's no copy, I like to listen to podcasts. That eve-

ning I was listening with tremendous excitement to the Tim Ferris Show interviewing Seth Godin, whose book The Icarus Deception blew my mind from a creative artist point of view. The story was very similar to your relationship with Herb. Tim Ferris ask Seth Godin, and I'm paraphrasing: Who helps tell you you're wrong? Or point out when your work isn't good? Who do you lean on when you need bitter truth? Seth answers Tim: So, I would break this into two kinds of people, and I have been blessed by being surrounded by very skeptical people, individuals who turned to me in 1991 and said the internet thing was never going to amount to anything. But the other kind is so scarce, so rare, so precious that I only get little dribs of it now and then. That is someone who gets you, someone who can see right through to your soul. Who, with generosity and care, can look you in the eye, hand you back something and say: I think this would be better if you did it again. And I had a business partner who was like that and finding that again in a consistent way is really precious ... and really hard[7].

Larry agrees completely. "Now, I kept looking for the next Herb. And what I kept encountering over and over again was that I was perceived as too threatening and intimidating to people. So, now here's Jim and he's maybe 69, 70 years old although he doesn't look it. The point is when we started doing business together, it was the furthest thing from my mind to get to this place where he yesterday said, 'We make a good team.'

"So, the whole point, to answer your question – and we touched upon this in the last chapter on why is this happening to me now – the answer really is that whatever the this is

7  Ferris, Tim "The Tim Ferris Show." Audio blog #138 [1:43:32]. *How Seth Godin Manages His Life — Rules, Principles, and Obsessions*. Publisher, Tim Ferriss. http://bit.ly/2R3m1jT. February 10, 2016.

that you're asking the question about, it's always going on. But are you paying attention? Now, if you're not paying attention, you'll miss it. In other words, even that epiphany I just had about meeting Herb is the result of us writing the book.

"So now you're back to the Buddha and the student," Larry starts telling a parable. "And the student says to the Buddha, 'Can you show me where God is?' And the Buddha says back to him, 'Can you show me where he isn't?' So this is always the way it's supposed to be, every single bit of it. That's the whole point of divine order."

I tell Larry about a similar story I read in Joseph Campbell's book The Hero's Journey where there's an awesome little story that Daisetsu Teitaro (D.T.) Suzuki, the Japanese Zen Buddhist philosopher, brought up in one of his talks. He tells of a young man who asks his guru, "Am I in possession of Buddha consciousness?" The guru said no. So the young man said, "Well, I heard that all things are in possession of Buddha consciousness, the stones, the trees, the flowers, the birds, the animals, and all beings." "Yes," said the master, "you are correct. All things are in possession of Buddha consciousness, the stones, the flowers, the bees, but not you." The student asked, "Why not me?" His guru answered, "Because you're asking the question. (Campbell, 2003, p.152)"

Larry laughs and says, "Exactly."

## Universal Insight:

*Nothing is wasted in God's economy.*
*Everything is EXACTLY the way it is supposed to be.*

# CHAPTER ELEVEN

# The Impact of the Goodman

*Accept what is, let go of what was, and have faith in what will be.*

**Sonia Ricotti**

I wanted to know what inspired Larry to take this path. He said, "(It was) my first, take-my-breath-away realization that the impact a person can have is beyond his wildest imaginings. I was lecturing at a Parker Seminar in Atlantic City. When I finished my talk, this beautiful young lady chiropractor introduced herself and said, 'I'm sure you don't know who I am but you're the reason I'm here; you're the reason I'm here as a chiropractor.' She proceeds to tell me this story. When her mother was pregnant with her, her mother developed lower back pain. She became a patient of mine in my chiropractic practice at that time. After she was born, her mother still had the back pain, different but less often, a little more often because of carrying her baby on one hip. The young lady said to me, 'So for the first almost five years of my life, at least every week or two, I was in and out of your office. All I knew was that whatever was wrong with you, you go see Dr. Goodman and he'll fix it! So when I was trying to decide what I wanted to do with my life, I couldn't imagine doing anything else but being just like Dr. Goodman and being in the place where people went for whatever was wrong in their lives to get fixed.'"

Larry says, "I just stood there. I swear to you, Martin, I got goosebumps again now just thinking about it. It took my breath away, number one, but number two, I swear to you that you have no idea what the impact is that you're having, no idea at all.

"And just so you know where you are in this evolution," Larry tells me, "I don't know what Mel (a client and friend I referred to Larry) is going to create, but whether she tells you or not, you have already had a global impact on her life. I don't want you to miss the impact that you have had by inspiring her to come to see me."

It's interesting, the affinity I've had to chiropractors since I was a little kid. My siblings and I always went to the neighborhood chiropractor. I would wake up with a sore throat, my mother would call Dr. Grusky's office, and we would get the first appointment at 7:15 a.m. I was back in school and feeling great again by 8:15 a.m. As a teenager I admired Dr. Grusky because he was always on vacation every other month. I remember telling him that. He said, "Martin, what would you like to do when you grow up?" I remember saying out loud: an architect. He said, "Well, you can be an architect of the spine," pointing to his posters of spinal cords spread across the wall. That still reverberates clearly in my mind to this day.

Larry interrupts and says, "Now, listen. You can be the chiropractor of people's business. You can be the place to go for whatever isn't working right in their business." He continues with sternness in his voice, "I swear to you, and I know that you've never seen that possibility in that way. If you can see it and re-give it form and re-give it structure and we monetize correctly, you can build a unique niche and go global with it. Because I promise you no branding, graphic arts, music lyrics and all the combinations of things you love to do ... nobody has ever thought of it as being the chiropractor for their business. What a chiropractor does is remove the interference so that the body and mind can do what the body and mind were designed to do, so that you can be as healthy and fully expressive of your potential as possible."

Larry reminds me, "If you're always marketing, you keep the demand in excess of your ability to supply. Then you get to pick and choose your clients, set your price point, and set yourself free of the desperation that's called striving. I should know because I'm an overnight success 60 years in the making. Pay attention to the bread crumbs that are out there for you; you just have to pick them up. Listen to your intuition and go with it."

## Universal Insight:

*The Law of Action: Action brings results, manifesting different results, depending upon our thoughts, dreams, emotions and words.*

# CHAPTER TWELVE

# The Goodman Factor
# Secret Handshake

*We can't create a new future while we're living in our past. It's simply impossible.*

**Joe Dispenza**

"When I taught my first seminar in Sweden 1993, I made a statement that that still holds true and still accurate today," Larry says. "If Jesus were alive today, he'd be a motivational speaker, he'd have webinars, he'd have a theme song, and he'd have a logo."

Absolutely, I agree, and he would be Instagramming, Facebooking, streaming online and gathering a list. So you're saying hypothetically in our modern day there are many forms of Jesus like a Tony Robbins of our time?

"Yeah, Tony Robbins, Werner Erhard, Dr. John Demartini, Napoleon Hill, Larry Goodman and anyone who that speaks to," Larry says. "In fact, the whole point of The Goodman Factor is to recognize your inner good MAN! The Goodman Factor is, and the whole point of the interaction starts with: What do you want?

"So listen, space-time repetition breeds mastery, and I've spent hundreds of hours speaking before hundreds of people. Here's the way the Universe is constructed related to business.

Remember me telling you the whole purpose to having a business is to see the laws of the Universe at work? And the purpose of having it thrive is so you get to know who you are and what your God-given talents are, to get to really own them, truly live with them and get to be comfortable with them? That is the whole point of the human experience, and that's The Goodman factor actually. It's who you are, why you are here.

"What are the set of talents that the creator gave you?" Larry asks. "Once you identify them, what do you want to do with them? What do you want to do with them that will be of service to others? You then monetize that answer so it will take care of you and the people you love. In the material world in which we live if you can't make money with it, it isn't going to be saleable. And if it isn't saleable you're not going to be able to inspire anyone else to be like you. That's the reason why you've got to thrive.

"Now you see vibrationally, energetically and even electro-physiologically, that's the truth. All a cell phone is, all a smart-phone is, is an extension of your nervous system. It allows you to be sensitive and to pick up information, from frequencies in the spectrum of the neural system that you came with from the factory— that being in your body— can't receive. So, we had to evolve this tool to let the unseen and the unheard be seen and heard through the tool, and that's it."

Speaking of vibrations, Larry reminded me of something I read from a book called *Frequency* by Penny Peirce[8], which is about reaching a Magical Turning Point. I read to Larry this paragraph because of the impact it had on me and to hear his

---

8 Peirce, Penny. Frequency: The Power of Personal Vibration. Beyond Words, 2009. Pg. 100.

feedback. Peirce explains, "You've been clearing your unhealthy habits and learning to raise your personal vibration. As you reach the crescendo of this clearing phase of the transformation process, life can become intense and chaotic and sometimes look hopeless. The old isn't working; you may feel self-sacrificing, unimaginative, and unable to move forward. You've shifted the emphasis just enough from fear to love that your old reality has destabilized, and the new reality of your soul is starting to break through. At this point, your life may malfunction, and you may have to let go of goals, possessions, people, or parts of your lifestyle."

Larry interrupts and says, "Maximum evolution occurs at the border of support and challenge, exactly!"

I continue, "You may lose whole aspects of your identity, your motivation and direction, and your comfortable habits. It's important not to backtrack into more fight-or-flight reactions. What's really happening is that your soul is saying, 'You are not this old, limited self anymore. It's time to discover who you really are and what you can do.' This is the point where the Phoenix lights itself on fire and mysteriously turns to gold."

"It's where you come face to face with the choice of who you really want to be," Larry says, "And that's The Goodman Factor, exactly right, that's it. In fact, that piece you just read, that's a flyer for the workshop. I couldn't have said it better myself.

"In fact, in the choice of the words and the energies of the words here is the difference between the choices of the words to describe a situation – shedding or losing[9]. Because when you

---

9 Free meme on Shedding or Losing at www.goodmanfactor.com/bookbonusmaterial

shed something it's implied that you don't need it anymore and you're fine without it, right? When you lose something – and this is part of the underlying secret to weight loss and why weight loss seems to fail – you feel incomplete, and you go looking for it, right? But what do you think happens when you try to lose weight? Think about it! You're holding on to what was. It's like you're holding on to your fat, and you wonder why the fat isn't going away when you exercise."

My God, everything is so interrelated, I tell Larry as I take a deep breath, as my own conscious starts connecting the dots.

Larry laughs and says, "What was it? There can be only one. That's what unity is, the way consciousness flows is from the one to the many, and then the way it is restored is from the many to the one. So when you go unconscious, your lower-minded consciousness says, 'Well, what about this? And what about that? And what about that and this? and blah blah blah.' And as your consciousness gets concentrated, all that's left is to say is, 'Okay yes, I understand, thank you.'

"I sent you that study of the relationship between the aging process and happiness," Larry says. "Literally it's not about the aging process, it's about accessing wisdom. How most people access knowledge is by the process of elimination. It's what left after you've already tried everything else. How does all this benefit Team Goodman? How does it help Martin's business? The principal is that it's easier to ride a horse in the direction it's already going.

"A contrarian is someone who attempts to oppose market forces whether in investing or in philosophy," Larry explains. "I used to be an avid body surfer. When you surf, the place where the ride is the best is not at the top of the wave but in the curl. The ride is the best there because everything is predictable. The challenge is to ride enough waves to know where the curl is and that ocean waves comes in sets. In market forces, economic cycles are real, so the challenge becomes reading the cycle and knowing where it's at in the business cycle. The difference between reading and getting it right, and learning it and getting it wrong, ahhh, therein lies where we're able to make laws gets to be such a lucrative prospect.

"What's the secret handshake?" Larry asks. "How do some people get these kinds of endorsements on the back of their book? How do they? How can they when I'm struggling to get all I can do just to pay my bills? They do it by hanging out in Starbucks in Coral Gables," Larry chuckles. "If you can't see the connection, it's because you're too close to the ground. It concerns vision and altitude. The higher your altitude, the more you are able to be detached from cause and effect. The more global your effect can be, the more you begin to recognize it's all an illusion, that it's all about you. When you under-promise and over-deliver, and you enable people to see a part of themselves that's more or better or different than what they ever thought they had, the only thing left to say is thank you."

## Universal Insight:

*Law of Cause and Effect: This law states that nothing happens by chance or outside the Universal Laws. For this law we look at every action. This is because every action has an appropriate reaction. Every action has a reaction or consequence, and we "reap what we have sown."*

# CHAPTER THIRTEEN
## The Seven Areas of Life

1. Spiritual

2. Mental

3. Vocational (Career)

4. Financial

5. Familial (Family)

6. Social

7. Physical

*Link all seven areas of life to your purpose*

*When the voice and the vision on the inside is more profound, and more clear and loud than all opinions on the outside, you've begun to master your life*

**Dr. John Demartini**

Not necessarily in that order but as described by Larry's mentor since 1992, Dr. John Demartini, the seven areas[10] we are to fulfill are our spiritual mission, our mental genius/creativity, vocational success/achievement/service, financial freedom/independence, our family love and intimacy/continuance of procreation, social influence and leadership, and our physical health/stamina, strength and well-being. Dr. Demartini explains, "So any area of life that we don't empower, somebody else will overpower. We are not victims of their over-empowerment, we are simply not empowered, and it is their over-empowerment that in turn initiates and catalyzes our drive for inner-empowerment."

"Interestingly enough," Larry says, "there are seven areas of life in the wheel the way John Demartini teaches it, and there are the same seven areas of life the way NET works through them at their success seminars, which was another one of those

---

10  For more in-depth understanding of the seven powers described by Dr. Demartini go to https://drdemartini.com/seven-areas-to-empower

happy coincidences."

I looked up the seven components of NET. They are emotional response, Pavlovian responses, repetition compulsion, memory and physiology, the meridian system, semantic system and muscle testing. All of which, in the single act of holding my arm up, brought up the seven sequences. My arm would fall in instances charged with emotion, called NEC and explained in chapter six. I cried, responded like a Pavlovian dog looking right and left, crinkled my nose right on cue. Fear and failure response meridians came up in full effect.

The seven areas of life are a catalyst to manifesting and guiding you to find your purpose and true authentic self, both in your personal life and business. By looking into each one of the seven areas one by one, you start looking inward instead of outward and not just in one area of your life but in all seven. You define your purpose and, in turn, this will help you be inspired and live your legacy. Writing them down and identifying your values within each of the seven areas with rhythms and balances will trigger rituals for long-term purpose. It will help you define the legacy you want to leave behind – your inner good-man. Clarify your desires and goals, determine the behaviors or qualities in alignment with your core values, and decide what you'd love to be, love to do and love to have. In all of the seven areas start applying your own good-man lifestyle. Live with gratitude. It's all about finding what Larry calls your "special sauce," which is the authentic you.

Now, grab a sheet of paper and draw a circle like my illustration. If you're a little more artistically savvy draw two circles to represent your bicycle wheel. Get creative with it; it's your wheel of life. Then, our bicycle tire needs seven spokes to keep it from collapsing, so draw in seven spokes. In my example, I used little text bubbles for my seven areas: spiritual, mental, physical, financial, career, family and social. The order is up to you.

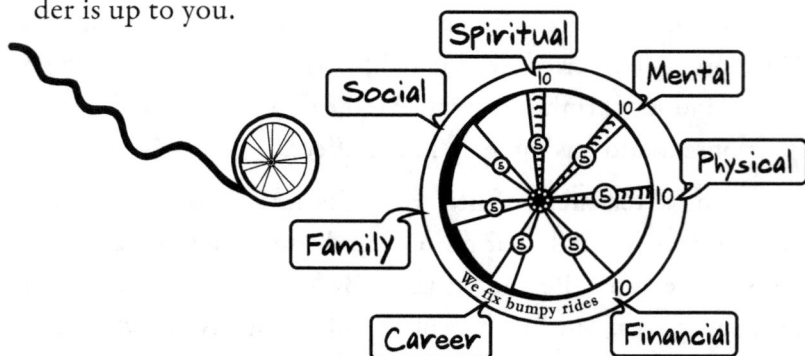

*Example illustration of "Life is like a wheel[11] "*

Larry explains, "From my understanding, most people live between a ten being the highest value and zero being the lowest value. Look at each area and assess yourself in each as far as fulfillment in your life from zero to ten. Then connect the dots on the spokes. The copy on the bottom says, "Life is like a wheel." and "How's yours rolling?" The tagline is, "We fix bumpy rides."

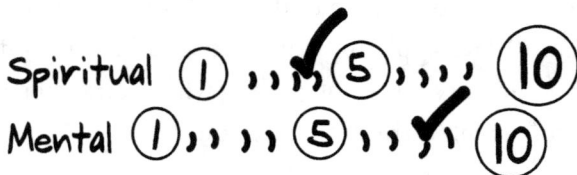

*Example Illustration of "Spokes from 1 to 10 in highest to lowest value"*

11  You can get a full diagram and PDF to fill out your own wheel at www.goodmanfactor.com/lifeislikeawheel

So within each spoke you would draw and put a 1, a 5 in the middle and a 10. Then, in-between each number, do four lines between the 1 and 5 and the 5 through 10. Then, circle – or in my example I checked it – where you think you're at within each increment between highest to lowest value.

This is an easy starter kit to understand the full assessment of the seven areas of your life. For each one of the seven areas, write down your be, do and haves as follows:

**BE:** "I would love to be....

**DO:** "I would love to do....

**HAVE:** "I would love to have...

### Number one, Spiritual:

Be: "Spiritually, I would love to be: _____

Do: "Spiritually, I would love to do: _____

Have: "Spiritually, I would love to have: _____

### Number two, Mental:

Be: "Mentally, I would love to be: _____

Do: "Mentally, I would love to do: _____

Have: "Mentally, I would love to have: _____

Continue down the list, as shown in these examples, for all seven areas of your life[12].

Then you can craft your affirmation in each area by managing statistics literally on what you write down and intuitively where your heart and your brain both agree. At least, that's how

---

12  You can get a full form and PDF to fill out your own BE.DO.HAVE sheet. at
   www.goodmanfactor.com/bookbonusmaterial

I approached this exercise. So my affirmation would look like this for my area of spirituality. I'd love to be fully self-aware and trust that the game is rigged, I can't fail, and everything is going to be okay. I'd love to do extra courses and read books by recognized teachers. Lastly, I'd love to have a Monday through Sunday tradition of all my spiritual practices at play. The wheel is an honest visual assessment of you yourself and a tool to let you see where you are in the present moment of your life. It's an exercise to visually clarify what is practiced by many teachers in various variations of the circle but using the same universal principles with their own topics. My wheel visual is part of the Demartini process taught to me by Larry.

Larry says, "The key to the seven divisions is they are a hologram for both your personal life and your business life whether you are self-employed or an employee of a large company. As an example, let's say what's missing from a person's life is a relationship. Now, part of why a relationship is most likely missing is because they never set about to package, market and promote themselves in that particular area. You see what I'm saying? In fact, a lot of what the literature is showing now is a downside to all of this internet-based, Facebook, social media and blah blah interaction. It is not only a poor substitute for face-to-face contact, but it allows people who are shy or suffer from low self-esteem to circumvent the process of pushing themselves through their own discomfort and growing as people because it's entirely possible to fill your time and even to have communication and interaction virtually."

BE. DO. HAVE. Larry continues, "When Demartini presents the process he calls it the Manifestation Formula.

Then, when it got submitted in the NET success workshop it was called 'building an atomic totem pole.' You know what a totem pole is in the Native American traditions? Each of these areas is a totem and the carving part is be, do and have. Only what you're carving it out of is the Universe instead of a piece of wood. The point is that your life is the piece of wood. You get to be the sculptor and designer of your life, except you didn't know it."

## Universal Insight:

*"I talk to myself with the respect due a great genius."*
*- Dr. John Demartini*

CHAPTER FOURTEEN

# The Energy of Money

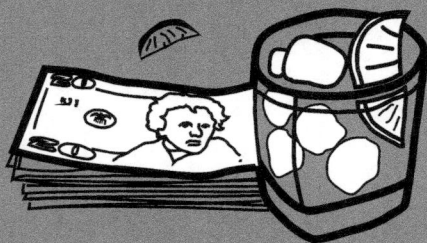

*My brain is only a receiver, in the Universe there is a core from which we obtain knowledge, strength and inspiration. I have not penetrated into the secrets of this core, but I know that it exists.*

**Nikola Tesla**

"So the bartender comes around and asks what you want to drink," Larry says. "Watch what happens. If I have a drink, not only is the tab going to go up but I am also probably going to feel like crap in the morning, which is going to make me feel more tired when dealing with that first client of the day. In turn, this is going to make my client feel he's receiving less value from me, which is going to make him less likely to refer another customer. This will then manifest in fewer referrals so that – watch this multiplier and I am not kidding! Let's just say the drink is $15. Now let's say a client can spend between $10,000 and $15,000 over the course of the year. You follow me? So how much is that drink? That is a $15,000 drink."

Wow, talk about perspective! I am guilty on all the above. It also reminds of something similar I catch myself often doing at your corporate chain coffee shops where I order many straight black coffees a week. I tell myself it is only $3 a coffee. Multiplied by sometimes twice a day, five to six times a week, for four weeks, that number starts to add up. That's not even adding the protein packs or bottles of water or the sometimes the cookie that I add to my order.

Larry interrupts, "Say that again because that is right on! That is the whole point."

Larry explained in one of our sessions that I had to re-craft my affirmations. Something that came up consistently was charging my worth when billing my clients. He suggested I craft my affirmations to always end with "... and be handsomely rewarded for it." An example of one of my recrafted affirmations is: Experiences that engage, connect and inspire my clients and be handsomely rewarded for it.

"The next piece that comes up for most people within my sessions has to do with the energy of money," Larry explains. "Most people have tremendous buttons around money. Like it is the root of all evil or the meek shall inherit the earth. I worked with a guy whose dad taught him that the only way to make a lot of money was to lie, cheat and steal. He thought that all rich people got their wealth by lying, cheating and stealing."

I tell Larry that my father used to say to me "always play poor." Go figure.

"So here's the point in the energy of money," Larry says. "There's a natural allocation system as to percentages of money to be allocated for each of the component parts of running your life. The millennials have convinced themselves that these are old school rules – that was then and this is now – and those rules do not apply. Moreover, that is why they cannot be self-sufficient."

I satirically say to Larry that they look great in their scarfs and fedoras in the hot summer's days in Miami.

He continues, "Well, yes. If you knew that discipline would set you free, watch what happened today. My daughter tells me that she and her boyfriend are going to move into together. They found an apartment on the same floor in her building. Now it gets better. They will both end up spending less on rent than they're spending individually and, because she is my daughter and evidently he was raised similarly, they are each going to start designated saving accounts. Because a luxury once tasted becomes a necessity."

If you want to have open lines of communication with your kids, one of the more positive role models is called "unconditional positive regard." Whatever is going on with your child, you convey, "I love you. If you feel it is the right thing to do, it is the right thing to do. If you start to feel that it is the wrong thing to do, I am here for you. I am open to discussing it with you, and I will help you sort it out." Larry tells me that is not the way he was raised, and I can relate. I was raised by my father who primarily said "This is the only way to do it. If not, you are stupid just like your mom."

"Back to the point about the energy of money," says Larry. "Money is just part of the cosmogonic system. Money is there to teach you the same universal laws, except we have made up all this crazy stuff about money. The negative programming started within the history of money, but that would just take too long to explain. However, I will sum it up for you this way. The greater the separation in time and space between the consumption and the payment, the more celebrated the detachment and the easier it is to violate the laws of supply and demand."

Something I experienced in my struggle with the association of money and my ego has been to prove myself to my father. After branching off on my own from a comfortable, stable life with all the conveniences, I created an alter ego of making it on my own through many trials and errors. I wanted to go back and defiantly say to him, "Look at me now. I told you so. I am a man, and I made it." Yet, I do not feel that anymore nor do I have the need to prove to my father or anyone for that matter that my journey worked. I mean, a past me was scripting the perfect words to say, painting some heroic scene of triumph, "I told you so and you should have believed in me." I do not feel that way anymore. In fact, I feel compassion and a need to give back and teach others like Larry taught me. I am different now.

Larry explains, "Well, because what you said to yourself does not matter. What matters is the awareness. That is the battle between ego and the creator because the ego wants to say 'See, I was right' and you, the co-creator, is humbled by the fact that it is the way that it is.

The test is always to have, what they call even in yoga,

'the beginner's mind.' You should always feel as if everything is new. That is how you get to create every day like it's the first day of the rest of your life. Now, when you do that the irony is the Universe rewards you with even more. Not less but more. Because the Universe gets the sense that you are a good receiver and you will be a good steward because that is part of what you do to demonstrate that you are learning the principles. This is the way you get more. Not by grabbing more, not by taking more and not by trying to make more happen, but by letting more happen."

## Universal Insight:

*A luxury once tasted becomes a necessity.*

# CHAPTER FIFTEEN

# I'm the Shit. I'm a Piece of Shit.

*Questioning illusions is the first step in undoing them.*

**A course in miracles**

A couple of weeks ago I experienced the hundredth monkey effect with my Instagram account, the one I do for Larry in which we both collaborate. I have a number of books, YouTube videos, articles and other information sources. I take a photo of something that inspires me and write small reviews on my account called martinsjourney. On Larry's Instagram, drlarrygoodman, he sends me a meme or a quote, and I write a review based on the topic. I base the keywords from his meme's inspiration and create the proper hashtags to promote The Goodman Factor. Instagram started letting the user manage multiple accounts. I had my personal account I used for artsy shots, but I always wanted to start others. Now I have my personal artsy one, my book savvy club one, one for my design company and drlarrygoodman. To tell you the truth, I had secretly been competing against myself with Larry's account and martinsjourney. Larry burst out laughing when I explained to him my social media experiment. I just can't beat you, Larry, I said, laughing too. Granted, martinsjourney posts weekly, sometimes monthly, and drlarrygoodman posts every day. I am experimenting with hashtags and playing the field equally, and I can't pass him! Then Instagram added a new feature similar to Facebook where you can see "people you may know" and boom! From 98 I went up to 200 followers and surpassed his account. Yet, I didn't want victory like that because I was trying to establish a community based on like-minded hashtags and a culture that was different from who I used to be.

Again Larry laughs at the thought of my ego playing the role it plays. He asks, "So, remember we talked about non-attachment to the outcome?"

Yes, I remember, but this just hit me out of nowhere, and it froze me.

He explains, "It feels like it 'froze you,' as you call it, because of your ego. It only appears like it froze you because you harbor the illusion that the material world experiences reality. Your experience with reality is just generated by the frontal cortex, and it's a whole holographic hallucination. So if you read A Course in Miracles about which Marianne Williamson and all the others talk about how the material world is an illusion, that's the neurophysiological basis for constructing the illusion. What they call in A Course of Miracles the 'ego thought system' is the stuff that uses the God part of the brain in the amygdala to generate the illusion. Also, which delusion it generates, and what the features of that illusion are, are always congruent and consistent with your thoughts, your belief system and your personal laws. Which is the experiential reason behind the universal law that what you fear comes near. You create it, you attract it, and you become it or its converse in which what you think and thank you bring about. Therein becomes your tipping point of attachment. Because when you are attached to the outcome and your ego says, 'There's no right, there's no good, there's no bad, there's just how it is,' it moves you closer to the construct that you have in mind. So to the extent that it works for you, you say, 'Oh I like this. Oh, I'm good. Thank you, God,' and then the ego kicks in and says, 'I'm the shit!'

"So here's the point. We live in the material realm under the delusion that who dies with the most toys wins. Like somehow that means something."

I interrupt and say that my ego was on the non-material way, kind of like "Oh man, the people who know me are going to find out another side of me."

Larry replies, "So another piece of the universal law is that everybody possesses traits. Every Being possesses every trait, meaning that in any given situation you can illicit any trait and any response from anybody. For instance, a starving mother with her starving child will kill, steal, lie and cheat. Remember the scene from Gone with the Wind where Scarlett O'Hara says something like, 'I'll do this, I'll do that, I'll do the other thing, but I will never go hungry again'? So, again, a master is someone who found out.

"Now, what happens as you achieve higher levels of (Larry

puts on his best Deepak Chopra voice) the cosmic conscious-ness? You get to see it, stand back from it and say, 'Hmmm, well that's interesting.' So the paradox of managing your business by statistics is that the purpose is to show you these universal laws in play. The purpose is not – and this is what happens to most of us especially in the beginning – to get the entire ego involved in the outcome. When the stats are going up we say, 'I'm the shit,' and when the stats are going down we say, 'I'm a piece of shit.'"

Larry concludes, "Just express thanks for your life on a daily basis. The secret is that there is no secret. Have fun, make money."

## Universal Insight:

*Every Being possesses every trait.*

---

The 100th Monkey[13] was explained in a book by Ken Keyes, Jr. In 1952, on the island of Koshima, scientists were providing monkeys with sweet potatoes dropped in the sand. The monkeys liked the taste of the raw sweet potatoes, but they found the dirt unpleasant. One of the females solved the solution by washing the potatoes in a nearby stream. It was like a domino effect of one teaching one monkey to another. Out of the monkeys on that spe-cific island within a span of about six years, the 100th monkey learned to wash the sand off the potatoes. There were colonies on other islands after that where monkeys started washing the sweet potato in water and it spread like wildfire. When a certain critical num-ber achieves awareness, this new awareness may be communicated from mind to mind.

---

13 Source: The 100th Monkey: A story about social change by Ken Keyes Jr.
http://www.wowzone.com/monkey.htm

# CHAPTER SIXTEEN

## Prisoner of Your Story

*Integrity is telling myself the truth.*
*And honesty is telling the truth to other people.*

**Spencer Johnson**

"So one billionaire says it's a rigged system and the other one says the game is stacked against you and the only way you can come out ahead is if we take the money from the rich and let the government redistribute it." Larry laughs and continues, "Can you see that that is only two sides of the same coin?" He was referring to a presidential election going on at the time this book was written.

I read somewhere, I tell Larry, that we only remember the last 24 hours instead of going back 50 or 100 years ago, that history repeats itself over and over again. So if you redistribute and give the government authority to assign the wrong responsibilities to the inexperienced people, we all lose.

"Completely," Larry agrees. "This is the principle of fair exchange and people's shame and guilt. What's part of what's going on right now on the planet regarding wealth is that when the children of the Great Depression raised their kids they gave them a sense of bizarre entitlement, and in that bizarre benefit they didn't teach them the laws of finance."

That's why you see now what Larry described to me as the universal self-correcting system in full effect. We're coming out of high school and some college, between 18 and 22 years old, waking up to the fact some simple things were not ingrained in us like the older generations had. We didn't learn the basics: taxes, savings and even critical thinking. This in turn leads to guys and gals flooding YouTube and social media online platforms picking up the slack. These "entrepreneur life coaches" are not backed by years of experience, if any, or any tangible assets.

"You got it,' Larry says, "and in conjunction with that you also have so many attention units to focus on being present in the moment. You can be present at the moment to be of service. You know Eckhart Tolle, The Power of Now, versus The Issues in Your Tissues by Denise Labarre, L.M.T.? So if the issues are in your tissues, let's just say we're having a conversation and that conversation triggers my unresolved issues. So in that conversation I'm like 70 percent working with you and with the other 30 percent I'm unconsciously churning up my stuff that's come up in regard, in response and in reaction to what is going on with you. One of the things that it's going to effect is my capacity."

Yes, I tell Larry, something was bothering me in one of our

sessions. I was conflicted within myself, in a complete mind fog. I was sitting in the chair telling you that I wanted to man the f—k up already. The truth is I keep saying I'm going to do all these things with my life. I keep saying I'm going to this and that, align my goals, assess my highest values. Then I am in my car taking care of my world and someone cuts me off, and I'm crazy mad! I curse to the world, and the truth of the matter is that my heart is no longer agreeing with my brain.

"The lesson you're bumping into," Larry says, "is that when the pain of staying the same is greater than the pain of change, that's when people change. It's a variant of the Law of the Lesser Pissers. As defined by Dr. John Demartini, this 'law' says that if you're given a choice between pissing someone else off or pissing yourself off, choose them. People come and go, but you're with yourself for the whole trip, and it's your life."

In this case, the pisser is within me. But how do we pinpoint that snapshot called the NEC (neuro emotional complex)? The trigger was when I said I wanted to man the f--k up, etc. It was an anxious, fear-induced need to make better decisions, and I can't come to terms with all that I'm re-learning.

"I call the synthesis of the Demartini process in combination with the NET 'pivotal moments,'" Larry says, "because in each area of life we've each got at least one pivotal moment, one major determining moment, and one snapshot that becomes the anchor where we make the rules about how we are related to the world related to that aspect. What happens is that sometimes we make up a story about that snapshot. And we believe the story that we made up is a fact, and we don't challenge that story.

"In fact, my personal mantra used to be 'You don't under-stand.'" Larry laughs and continues, "Whenever I would come face-to-face with my belief system and whatever had gone on in my life, my knee-jerk response was 'You don't understand.' Now, who do you think really didn't understand?"

You, of course, I respond to Larry. He says, "Right!" and laughs again.

"So when you get to the snapshot, the Demartini appli-cation is that since nothing happened in your life that didn't ultimately serve you, what was the benefit of that? What was the blessing of that?" Larry asks. "What's the benefit in learning to, as you say, man the f—k up?"

I ask Larry when he raises my arm up in the NET pro-cess, how does he pinpoint with such accuracy my age where he could capture my neurological response?

"Well, that's when your neurology says you got locked in. When you're stressed to the max what you get is fear 'flight or freeze' and mostly what immobilizes us is the freeze part of it. What it feels like is just being stuck. In fact, haven't you had the experience where your internal dialogue says, 'I've got to do something. What the f--k is going on?' It almost feels like, at least for me, that somebody pulled the plug on the whole machine called my life. I can't say a thing, and I can't do a thing.

"I did a whole bunch of psychodrama work. Psychodrama is another tool where you take people in a workshop and act out the people who were present in your snapshot. It's a fasci-nating thing because when you act out the snapshot you can feel the paralysis. The point is you get to see and experience how you're a prisoner of your story. You literally take other people and position them to represent your snapshot, so you consciously know it's not them. When you clear your snapshot, then you get to claim your power back."

## Universal Insight:

*Law of the Lesser Pissers: If you're given a choice between pissing someone else off or pissing yourself off, choose them. People come and go, but you're with you for the whole trip, and it's your life. – Dr. John Demartini*

# CHAPTER SEVENTEEN

# S-O-R-T-I-N-G the Friends Process

*Somebody asked me if I knew you. A million memories flash through my mind, but I just smiled and said I used to.*

**Unknown**

Something that has been bothering me lately when talking with friends or acquaintances is seeing that when men find a formula to deal with money they forget about all the other six areas of life. Their balance is completely off. In the seven areas of life they've dominated the "financial area," but there is disorder in their physical, mental and relationship areas. I can sense in their sarcasm and cynical demeanor that they are just going through the motions. What I recognize is that the ego is so intoxicated with getting money that friends I've known for a long time never took the time to look into themselves. And those friends seem to be the most judgmental!

Larry responds, "Well, because in a capitalistic system we tend to view our state of well-being as being related to the bank balance."

My ranting continued. I've changed and invested strongly in myself. My values and outlooks in evaluating my own life have matured. I am not the same Martin from 2013. I used to spend so much time pleasing others that I didn't even know who I was. The more I let myself dive deep into my self-mastery, the more I enjoyed my own company and didn't need to be so social anymore. A quote that resonates with me is by the Buddha, "It is better to be alone than to be with those who hinder your progress." Some friends took it very personally, but the right ones are still around.

"Upon discovery you see the friend thing come into play," Larry says. "Look up the poem A reason, a season or a lifetime. (See below.) It's a S-O-R-T-I-N-G process. Think of a coffee filter. When you make coffee, you pour in some water. Next, you have the filter, then the coffee grounds. After the process is done, what you have underneath the filter is the coffee and above the filter are the grounds. Now you don't lament the grounds, do you? You have to go through that process to wind up with the coffee."

I was watching a show on Netflix called Chef's Table. It's an amazing show, so well-produced, that showcases the lives of award-winning chefs. One in particular, Francis Mallman[14], a famous Argentine chef, talked about friends we outgrow. Francis said (and I'm paraphrasing), "I had this friend of mine in Patagonia, Argentina where I grew up, in fact, 30 years ago when we just started, and we parted you know. We just went different ways in our lives. Once he came back to me and said, 'Francis, you don't like me anymore.' And I said that it's not that I didn't like him,

---

14  Mallmann, Francis. "Chef's Table - Season 1, Francis Mallmann, Netflix." Creator David Gelb, V1:E3, Minute 29:20, Netflix, 8/16/2015, https://goo.gl/nVxAhv.

we had chosen different styles of life. I still have these beautiful souvenirs of all the things we did together and how close we were and so on. But the truth is, it's not that he bored me, I didn't enjoy talking to him anymore. I didn't want to fight with him but there was nothing in common between his life and mine. I would have never said that to him, but he asked me so what can I say, I said the truth. But you know growing up has a bit to do with aptitudes, being able to tell the truth, to show who you are, even if it hurts." I tell Larry that this is how I have been feeling about some friends.

"Yes, and the other thing about that is you tell the truth if it's asked for," Larry says in response to my reaction to Francis' story. "There is a difference between meddling and helping. Meddling and judging are giving your opinion whether it's asked for or not. The whole engagement process that I go through with people is necessary for the purpose of creating the magic. Without the engagement, the wall of judgment and criticism won't come down. What goes on in judgment and criticism, because it's not solicited, is that the ego basically says something like 'Who the f--k are you?' and/or 'I didn't ask for your opinion' and/or 'Just what the hell is it that you've done that gives you the right to tell me that?'

"This is why when I'm working with you or anybody else I don't say 'You need to do whatever.' Because the truth is that whatever people do they do and unless they're dead, you know, physically dead, what they're doing is working. It just may not be creating the result that they want, which is why they come see people like me. They've gotten feedback from life that they'd like to have a different outcome. So I don't tell anybody they have to anything because they don't. They could. They might. What I would do if I were you is .... What if you ...? In other words, giving people choices is where the empowerment lives. What people do with those options is very variable. Mostly, what you truly see and analyze, at least in my experience, is that you can and will outgrow people, and that's perfectly okay."

**The Poem:**

*People come into your life for a reason, a season or a lifetime.*
*When you figure out which one it is,*
*you will know what to do for each person.*

*When someone is in your life for a REASON,*
*it is usually to meet a need you have expressed.*
*They have come to assist you through a difficulty;*
*to provide you with guidance and support;*
*to aid you physically, emotionally or spiritually.*
*They may seem like a godsend, and they are.*
*They are there for the reason you need them to be.*

*Then, without any wrongdoing on your part or at an inconvenient time,*
*this person will say or do something to bring the relationship to an end.*
*Sometimes they die. Sometimes they walk away.*
*Sometimes they act up and force you to take a stand.*
*What we must realize is that our need has been met, our desire fulfilled; their work is done.*
*The prayer you sent up has been answered and now it is time to move on.*

*Some people come into your life for a SEASON,*
*because your turn has come to share, grow or learn.*
*They bring you an experience of peace or make you laugh.*
*They may teach you something you have never done.*
*They usually give you an unbelievable amount of joy.*
*Believe it. It is real. But only for a season.*

*LIFETIME relationships teach you lifetime lessons;*
*things you must build upon in order to have a solid emotional foundation.*
*Your job is to accept the lesson, love the person,*
*and put what you have learned to use in all other relationships and areas of your life.*
*It is said that love is blind but friendship is clairvoyant.*

– Unknown

# CHAPTER EIGHTEEN

# Breathing Out My NEC
# (Neuro Emotional Complex)

*Enlightenment consists not merely in the seeing of luminous shapes and visions, but in making the darkness visible. The latter procedure is more difficult and therefore, unpopular.*

Carl Jung

Okay, let's continue to walk through my NET experience. We're back at the moment when Larry holds my arm up and brings up the inception of "manning the f--k up." My arm falls at the age of 17 years old. He asks me, "Where are you at 17 years old?" I couldn't recall whether there's a girlfriend in my life at that time, my father, financial, or who's know what. Because, remember, I'm 39 years old and that was 22 years ago. To help me focus on the actual event, I held out my arm again. I was saying, "My girlfriend Maria, my friends, my mom, my dad." Larry was saying, "No, no, not that, that ... that's it!" when my arm fell when I said "my father." How did you do that? I asked him.

"It's too much to explain right now," Larry answers. "It is the reason why they only teach NET to licensed health care practitioners, as opposed to PSYCH-K where they'll teach it to anyone. The precision requires a level of training and sensitivity that John Q Public doesn't have. Think about somebody who is an entertainer and uses hypnosis versus someone who's a clinician who uses hypnosis. One's a parlor trick, and the other one is deep and profound, personality-changing therapy. And in the parlor trick you can't hypnotize somebody to make them do anything that their unconscious doesn't want to do. In the parlor trick realm it's completely safe to hypnotize when there's an audience around. When it's done on stage you don't get down into the depth of the psyche because the unconscious knows to keep those walls up."

Okay, continuing with the NET session. We pinpoint it's a father issue and I'm 17. Larry says, "So then it becomes the seven areas of life, and then there's a whole semantic string that comes from NLP, and that's how you drill down to get to the root of it. Sorry for using so many acronyms. NLP means Neuro-Linguistic Programming. What we're doing is accessing the operating system of your body/mind bio-computer. It's the language of the software of your mind. What's happening now is that science is catching up. With functional MRIs they can see the regions of the brain that light up in response to either the image or the description of that snapshot (NEC)."

So we narrowed down my NEC, my snapshot, to when I was 17 and about to graduate high school. I wanted to study graphic design or some creative endeavor. What I wanted wasn't going to happen because my dad told me I was going to study finance. That was one NEC I had been living with for so long, unconsciously and consciously aware, acknowledging that time in my life.

Larry explained, "So the first part is you have to find out what you're stuck in. The second part is to forgive yourself for being stuck in it. The third part is to locate the blessing in being stuck in it. The last part is to be grateful for the stuck-ness. And that's transformation. If you semantically break up the word trans-form, you'll understand what's going on in life. You're forming a trance, a quasi-hypnotic trance, except you forgot that you made it up, so you're living like it's true."

In the process of acknowledging my 17-year-old self with my father and college decision-making, I am acutely aware in my present adult mind of the situation that outwardly affected me to my present day. Larry and I sit knee-to-knee, and he asks for my opposite arm. With his other hand, he feels beneath my palms in the tendons of my wrist. He then places one of my fingers from my other hand on a precise tendon in my wrist where it meets my palm. Next, he asks me to place my hand over my forehead while still holding my wrist and finger upon that one tendon.

Larry explains, "Those points on your forehead are called emotional neurovascular points and they fit right on top of the prefrontal cortex. The prefrontal cortex, we now know from brain mapping, is where the hologram of reality is created in your mind. That's what lets you press the delete key on the emotional charge on that hologram so that it goes from being a significant emotional event to just being an event. That's when you can move on. That's when you can use the language 'get over it' because when the charge dissipates there's nothing to get over. It would be like my telling you to get over whatever you wore yesterday. Unless you had some superstition of what you were wearing yesterday, your conscious mind is going to say, 'What is this guy talking about? I don't even remember what I wore yesterday.' To your mind there was nothing significant about it. Now, if you were a baseball pitcher, whom I consider the most superstitious athletes I know, things would be different. Pitchers in baseball assign significance to weird shit, a lucky T-shirt, a lucky sock, whatever. They create a link between an outcome and a moment. They make the snapshot, and instead of it being unconscious they keep it conscious, and they build a superstition about it."

Okay, but let's get back to the NET[15] process. I am holding my hand on my forehead still with my other hand and finger on the tendon. Larry asks me to remember the original 17-year-old moment while breathing in the faith of the blessing and coming to terms with the outcome. He guides me through the process of healing by breathing deep breaths and exhaling out what no longer suits me. I go through this process of breathing deeply and long until I feel this feeling of stability. I guess the best way to describe the feeling is a neutral calmness in the mind.

Larry says, "So just put this into your computer (referring to my thoughts) and play with this for a second. You know why smoking is so addictive? It's not the tar, it's not the nicotine, it's the forced rhythmic breathing. You're teaching a rhythm of breath to people who have no conscious awareness of their forced rhythmic breathing. When they try to stop smoking it's like denying themselves a fix. That's the reason why one of the things they wind up doing is overeating. Once you see what's going on behind the curtain, your life is never the same because you can't pretend anymore that you don't know."

After I breathe, I let it all out, lower my hands and relax my arms. Lastly, Larry has me hold up my arm once more just to see if the process is complete. Then he jots down on your pad with some notes. I ask him what he ends up with.

"If I tell you I have to kill you," Larry laughs. "You have to understand that you're asking me a question related to something that I've only been doing since 1992. And not only since

---

15 Our NET Effect is Changing the World. In ONE Research Foundation.
Retrieved from http://www.onefoundation.org/

1992 but next week when I'll be with Demartini and some of the greatest leaders and experts in the world on it, I'll come back with another layer. The highest level of spiritual awareness related to being present in the now, to borrow from Eckhart Tolle, is to be okay with a thing just the way it is and that's what you're checking. And that's literally the power of now."

## Universal Insight:

*I am never upset for the reasons I think I am.*
*Whenever I have a two-pound reaction to a one-ounce*
*current event, it's never that event.*

# CHAPTER NINETEEN

# Risk Reward Ratio vs. Student Loans

Miami International Art & Design

Martin Casado

Miami International Art & Design Miami International Art & Design

*Don't be too timid and squeamish about your actions. All life is an experiment. The more experiments you make the better.*

**Ralph Waldo Emerson**

Coming from a family company, you get to a certain age where you ask yourself, "Is this what I'm supposed to be doing?" In my many attempts to finish a college degree in business, I never followed through because I had to attend to the family business. Honestly, this was all I knew. In between hating being stuck in a warehouse managing truck drivers and warehouse receipts, dealing with secretary drama within the office and working Wednesdays and Fridays until sometimes 1 or 2 a.m., you start to question your life. My solution was to pursue creative independence from my family company, and my answer was to get a bachelor's degree in graphic design. At 27 years old I decided that a degree was the answer to getting out of this continuous loop called "doing what's expected of you." I had no desire to get a Master's degree but at the very least have a bachelor's degree under my belt. That's the way I saw it at the time. Not a business degree or finance degree, like my father wanted me to do at 17, but a Bachelor of Arts degree in graphic design. You know. Do what you're good at. A $70,000 resume filler with a minimum of two years' experience plus those student loans that kick in just six months after you graduate.

As Larry would put it, "Nothing goes wasted in God's economy. There is a divine order, and everything happens for a reason." On that first day I met him I was whining about having these student loans going straight out of my account every month. The loans never go down, and if I had only known this before, I would have reconsidered. I felt trapped, and there are only so many years you can defer the payments. Then Larry stopped me in mid-sentence and told me, "No, Martin, you made that decision to get that degree. You signed the student loan agreement." I continued to say that was the way we were all taught. To get the better job you wanted and be able to support a better lifestyle, you get another degree or, better yet, a master's degree.

"Here's another paradox for you," Larry says. "You are a unique child of God with your own magnificent set of talents and you're nothing special. You came equipped from the factory with the same basic software package and the same basic hardware package as everybody else. The point about that is not to be so hard on yourself about the fact that you got sucked into this thing, because it was designed to suck you in.

"Remember that thing I sent you, the survivor course for the millennials[16]?" Larry asks. "The reason this course needs to exist is that the baby boomers dropped the ball. Most of them did not teach their kids the things that used to be taught by a

---

16 To watch the Millennial International: Sponsor a Millennial Today go to www.goodmanfactor.com/motivationalads or watch it at - http://bit.ly/2rCS385

parent. I remember the conversation I had with my dad. He said, 'So you want to go school, and you want to get that degree? Okay, now what are you going to do with it? What's it going to cost you to get it? How long? And what are the career earning potentials on the other side?' Nowhere in that conversation were thoughts like, 'It interests me.' or 'It's my passion.' In fact – this is funny, and I haven't thought about this in a while, but it's connected – when it was decided that my younger brother was going to medical school, I wrote his essay to get him accepted. This is a guy who has the least empathy and the least connection with his inner self. You would not see him and say, 'This guy is a healer.' I remember having this conversation with my dad about what happens if, after he gets there, he doesn't like it. You know what my dad's answer was? My father said, 'If he doesn't like it after he gets there, he can always be something else. Having your MD is great to fall back on in case things don't work out.' And so the specialty he chose was anesthesiology because then you don't have to deal with the people – you knock them out."

In one of our Friday sessions Larry told me that when he told his father what he wanted to do, his father said he was going to call his accountant to see what this chiropractic business was all about and what their salaries were. Then that required an x, y, z formula to understand what the student loan would be, in how many years would it be paid off based on the income Larry would be receiving and so forth.

Larry says, "There is a whole formula, and most people didn't get trained about it anymore. When I got it explained to me, the guy who taught it to me labeled it 'f--k you money.' Are you familiar with the concept? It's basically having enough money to support your desired lifestyle without needing help from anyone. So when you make a career choice, you make the return on investments (ROI) figure into it because of this factor."

I continue to talk to Larry about the question of finding my purpose or of finding my passion and never "working" another day in my life when I'm working at what I enjoy. Sometimes, I wonder where I would be if I hadn't read The Power of Myth by Joseph Campbell, self-improvement books, business books, seminars online, YouTube content on people I value and the multiple inspirational quotes like "When I let go of what I am, I become what I might be" by Lao Tzu. I often feel I manifested where I am today from going this route. The common theme among self-help books or "personal development books" was leaving the corporate hamster wheel or a successful family company only to fail multiple times and, sometimes, almost losing it all, e.g., selling everything, moving into a studio apartment and eating ramen noodles before figuring it out. And that's not counting the other seven areas of life. I followed my path, and I triumphantly got my ass kicked. I followed my bliss, and I failed many times because I had to learn this new paradox in which the old ways no longer suited me.

"Yes, because that's what the new consciousness is calling for," Larry says. "Because the new consciousness means you don't have to sell out. If you knew what you really love – really love – you could do what you love and love what you do and be magnificently compensated for it. That's where The Goodman Factor and coaching came into play. It was, 'Okay, this is what I love to do, now how do I monetize that?' You just need guidance.

"Now, when you learned how to conduct business it was all in the family, it was all designed to be kept a secret. So here is a story for your entertainment and amusement. At the turn of the 20th century when D.D. Palmer discovered chiropractic and began his clinic, it was going to be the family business. Don't laugh at this; go ahead, just try not to. The first thing he did was take down the mirrors in the treatment rooms. He didn't want the patient to see what he was doing because the patient might figure it out and teach it to somebody else, and that would rob his lineage of its legacy. When his son came along, his son, the entrepreneur, went to business finishing school. He said, 'Listen, forget about just making it a family business. Let's build a school. Let's turn them out by the hundreds. Then they will keep coming and create a perpetual income stream.' The Law of the Lesser Pissers is right there."

Larry explained that the risk reward ratio affects your perception of your life. "The greater the risk that's at stake for the less the reward, the greater is your perception of being under stress. The greater the reward for the less at risk, the greater your perception of fun. And that's the nature of the beast. If you don't always keep an eye on the bottom line, that sucker can get away from you and you can wind up in that tail-wagging-the-dog scenario.

"Here's how relative this is," Larry explains. "My brother went to school with a guy whose family owned diamond mines in South Africa. They met at the University of Colorado in Boulder, and they became roommates and friends. The guy's father fought him every step of the way because he felt that he was wasting his time getting a degree in management and economics. Even though the kid kept saying (A) it's what interested him and (B) it would help him grow the business even more, the father was like, 'What do you want to waste all this time for? I need you here to run the company now.' And they fought for years."

That sounded familiar. I told my father I wanted to study graphic design when I got out of high school. Right before graduating high school, my father said, "You're studying finance." I told my dad I decided to study graphic design, and my dad pretty much said, "No, you're studying finance." So that's what I did and I dropped out half way through.

"Watch this now," Larry said. "This is the relationship between voids and values and not having balance. Because he forced you instead of allowing you to discover its worth, you failed to take into consideration the principles of finance when you set up your own business."

Because I quit the family business, I took on a bachelor's degree with a big student loan, read those books and failed those many triumphs in running my own business, but I did meet Larry.

"Well, when the student's ready...."

## Universal Insight:

*Nothing you do means anything.*
*However, anything you do means everything.*

# CHAPTER TWENTY
## Analysis Paralysis

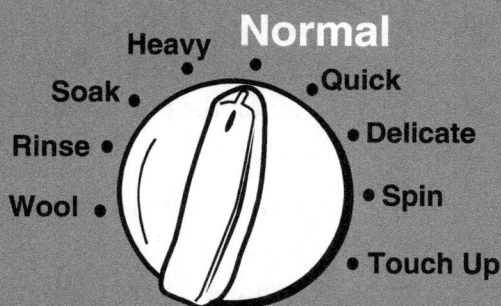

*We must remember that the power to direct our destiny comes only from a mindset that makes us willing to struggle through learning, effort, and growth.*

**Brendon Burchard**

One day, I got inspired when I was browsing online. A light bulb went off in my head when I saw the title of a book, which I had not read, called Tuesdays with Morrie. It's about an old man, a young man, and life's greatest lesson. I sent Larry an email and told him I had the title of our book we needed to write. Instead of Tuesdays with Morrie we would call it Fridays with Goodman. Larry wrote back saying, "Who you calling old man, buddy?"

The way the book evolved was by Larry's one-on-one coaching, the NET, Business Finishing School and his guidance in mentoring me, which changed my life in immeasurable ways. We meet every Friday at 9 a.m., and until this day, in the writing of this book, we still meet at that exact time. I am forever grateful. The learning curves we all have to go through in living an authentic life don't always go as planned. Like the expression goes, "We plan, and God laughs." That being said, the story became less about me (because that is how I started writing this story). I realized that not many would care about me writing about leaving my family company, my daddy issues and my "waa waa" victim-mode story. Who really had the experience and the heart was Dr. Larry Goodman. The star is Larry, and a privileged artist who went off on his own realized, as Socrates said, "I know one thing: that I know nothing."

"Well, you know," Larry says, "the whole point is there is the continuum of prepared, over-prepared, well-prepared, spontaneously prepared and 'fly by the seat of your pants.' So what you see in our experience, for example, is all of it intertwined. 'By the seat of your pants' does not work. That's one polarity. The other polarity that doesn't work is so over-prepared that everybody can tell that you're not authentic. In statistics, a standard distribution is a curve that looks like a bell curve. At the top end there's a little tiny slice and at the bottom end there's a little tiny slice. In the middle is where the normal range is. Normal is not just a setting on a washing machine, it's also not just a 'why be normal?' condition. In the normal range is what people are striving for, which is competence, planning but also still authentic and spontaneous enough so that when and if something comes along that requires spontaneity, you can draw from the wisdom and still deal with what you had not planned on encountering.

"Now this is the place where having your own values in place winds up to become so critical. If you don't have a sense of your own value system then when something comes along that is not what you planned for, you suffer from what they call analysis paralysis[17]. A person thinks, 'I don't know what to do. I never encountered this before. There's no way I can turn and look at these set of circumstances and come up with a clear answer because it's nothing I ever planned on encountering. So, I'm going to do nothing because I don't want to do the wrong thing.' They become paralyzed."

What about in the scenario of setting and having your values, but you don't like tasks they entail?

"Well, that's the point," Larry says. "If you don't have confidence and certainty in your values, in the viability of your values and in the faith that your values are consistent with the way the laws of the Universe operate, then spontaneity can be terrifying. Because what you get caught up in is: What if this? Well, what if that? What if that and that? So, by the time you've finished with enough of these 'what ifs,' the circumstances have changed again. You have a new problem to deal with, which now includes calculating in the effect of your lack of response to the situation that required in an immediate response.

"In life there is a breaking point. How do you get to that point without falling apart? What holds people back, ironically, is the fear of what would happen if they let go. There's a metaphor – not even a metaphor, it's truth – about a cookie jar. You have your hand in a cookie jar, and you have a handful of cookies in your hand. You will not be able to get your hand

---

17 Analysis paralysis or paralysis by analysis is the state of over-analyzing (or over-thinking) a situation so that a decision or action is never taken, in effect paralyzing the outcome.
Source: https://goo.gl/rbk7Dy

out of the cookie jar unless you let go of all the cookies and take them out one at a time. So if you have a sense of urgency about getting all the cookies out, then you get nothing. Well, if you hold on to the past because you're afraid to lose it, you close the door on your opportunities and your options for a better present and future. So take that for what it is."

I tell Larry that I use the same comparison that I call the juggling effect. Since I'm an experienced juggler, I always remind people who say they're juggling too many things in their life that there's always one ball in hand at all times.

"That's correct," Larry says. "When you can recognize that that is what it is: waking up. Then you can let go of the fear. There are two definitions of fear: f--k everything and run, or face everything and revise. There are many different ones, but the one that fits our story, organizationally and even in your life, is reviewing. That's really what you're doing. You are taking the parts, and you're going to use all the parts in a new and improved way. Like what I just said to you since the beginning: There's nothing wasted in God's economy."

## Universal Insight:

*The Universe abhors a vacuum.*
*Something or someone will show up to fill the void.*

# CHAPTER TWENTY ONE

# Catalyzing The Goodman Factor

*Remember that self-doubt is as self-centered as self-inflation. Your obligation is to reach as deeply as you can and offer your unique and authentic gifts as bravely and beautifully as you're able.*

**Bill Plotkin**

I told Larry we lacked a catalyzing statement for the book. As defined by Rick Sapio in the Business Finishing School course, that's "a phrase that allows everyone to visually see, in their mind's eye, exactly what you want to do while they also become emotionally attached to it." Everyone has their declaration of what inspired them to write their story. Mostly you hear they wrote their book because of an XYZ moment that changed their life forever and inspired them to share that experience. I say our catalyzing story is "a life's experience appearing in space-time to the student who was ready for The Goodman factor." Larry once suggested it was "to find out all your God-given talents and abilities and what it is you want to do on this planet." In my case, he helped me discover my deep-rooted inner blocks that clouded my present-day decisions and resurrected a purpose into my journey.

"Yes, my catalyzing statement is 'unleash your inner goodman,'" Larry says. I tell him I agree, but we need a universal truism for the experiences had by all the fortunate people who have sat in his chair.

"Okay, Martin, after X period of time of sitting with people in that chair, what became apparent to me was literally in every one of us there's an inner good man or good woman who wants to come out." Larry says. "Depending on how long it's been and how deeply buried it is, and sometimes I've had to be the one to tell them that it's in there. That is because they have been so alienated from it, so isolated from it, and put so many layers of negativity on it that they don't even believe me. I mean that sincerely; they don't even believe me. And so that becomes the place to say it. I've said that a lot of times to people, especially to the people who I wind up in a hybrid business relationship. One part of the relationship is to prove to them that I believe in them enough to do the joint venture with them. They have more faith in me than they do in themselves, and so I ask for them to take the faith they have in me and to believe that I believe in them."

At that moment I felt something. It was as if a weight lifted from my heart and I understood how much he believed in me. As he continued, I applied the most important lesson of all and that was to stay quiet and listen.

"So that's how deep the buried inner good man or good woman can be," Larry continued. "In fact, I just gave someone an assignment yesterday to make a list of all of the times things worked out even when they didn't think they would. Because, you see, that's the evidence that you have to force someone to recognize before they are even willing to believe that there's an inner good man or a good woman in there. Because when you self-sort to minimize your accomplishments and maximize your failures, you store up the evidence of how unworthy you are.

"So instead of being the master of persistence and perseverance and hanging in there because this too shall pass and nobody scores a hundred percent, what winds up happening instead is this. Imagine if in baseball every time the batter got a strike he threw the bat down and said, 'I suck. I quit.' You can see how ridiculous that could be, right? He could be in a slump. What happens in a slump is the person believes that what's going on right at that time, that negative situation, is somehow representative more of who they really are than the total picture, which is balance, symmetry, proportion and order. So if every time something doesn't turn out the way you think it's supposed to, you conclude that it's because you suck, what do you think is going to happen?

"There's a line in the big book of Alcoholics Anonymous that says, 'There are those poor unfortunate that seem to have been born that way. They are constitutionally incapable of being honest with themselves.' I remember getting on the plane to go to drug camp and thinking, 'If the plane crashes that's okay with me because I'm pretty sure this isn't going to work for me anyway because I'm one of those people.' This was where my mind was at that moment because I'd been called a liar so many times. Now, do you know how many times especially in the last two or three or four years I've had the epiphany of, 'Holy crap, if any of my little suicide attempts had been successful, look what I would have missed. Look at the life I would have missed. Look at the people whom I've gotten to reach and touch.' So the point is there is an inner good man or good woman in there, and don't believe anything you think."

## Universal Insight:

*The Universe rewards action and, even more than that, it rewards persistence.*

# CHAPTER TWENTY TWO

## The Antithesis of Humility

*If you want guarantees in life, then you don't want life.
You want rehearsals for a script that's already been
written. Life by its nature cannot have guarantees, or
its whole purpose is thwarted.*

**Neale Donald Walsch**

We've talked from time to time about negative motivators. I started to tell Larry about an article sent by a friend of mine who worked for a sociopath.

Larry interrupted me to talk about sociopaths. "You understand why some people think the only way they are able to achieve a level of success is by being a sociopath, right? A sociopath has no conscience. Actions have consequences. You need to make atonement for your errors. Atonement doesn't just mean owning up and saying, 'Yes I did it.' Atonement means taking ownership of the action and making a change in your way of doing things to prevent and minimize the likelihood of it happening again. Something you should look up is called aggrandizement, to make one's self larger than one is. This is the antithesis of humility."

"Okay, back to the sociopath," I say. "In the same sense of not having a consciousness, they motivate others in a way to find their purpose as well, right?"

"Well, here's the problem with a true sociopath," he continues. "There's a book called People of the Lie: The Hope for Healing Human Evil. This book is about sociopaths in your life and in the world. The problem with a sociopath isn't that they don't take ownership of their misgivings and misdeeds, it is literally that in their mind it's not a misdeed. It would be like if one of the chips got left out of your computer at the factory, and that chip was the 'conscious' chip. Because it's left out, there's no atonement because there's nothing to atone for. This is the hallmark description of the world from the eyes of a sociopath. I knew my first wife was a sociopath when she would say, 'I hate the things you make me do. I hate the things you make me feel.' Now, you see the problem with that is," Larry laughs.

"Absolutely," I say. "This is why I brought this up. I was reading that article my friend had sent me and I was like, 'Holy –! My father has sociopathic tendencies too!' They show in the article where at one moment everything is great, and then they will ignore you for days. When you finally bring it up again, that's when you give them permission to berate you and say hurtful things. That is exactly what's happening right now. We were supposed to meet on Monday for my birthday. I get a call from my sister that he doesn't want to do anything, so I should make other plans. He's mad at something I did; who knows what it is this time. We spoke the other day to see if he needed any help with the hurricane shutters, and we were amicable and fine. Now he's ignoring me for my birthday. Back to the article about the sociopathic tendencies where everything is cool, and then, well, that's what he's been doing to me my whole life. I don't know. That was just one of the many signs in the article that just hit a nerve."

"So my mother is the original sociopath in my life. When she would do emotionally abusive things to me, her explanation was, 'Well of course I did, because of what you did.' What?!" Larry exclaims, satirically dumbfounded. "Then when I wound up in drug camp, her explanation to the therapist was 'It's not like they had any books around to teach you how to raise a kid.'"

I remember reading somewhere in the book Conversations with God something very comforting on why our parents do these things that we don't understand, and they don't realize that they are doing. It was something along the lines of their parents taught them that and their grandparents did the same thing, and they're just passing down all they knew in this cycle of raising children.

"So when I had Alexa, my daughter," Larry continues, "my model for parenting her was like that line from an episode of Seinfeld, 'However my parents were to me, I'm going to do the opposite.' I didn't hear from my biological father since I was 12 – I talk to my daughter every day. My mother never took ownership of anything that she did in the way that she behaved toward me. I'm always asking my daughter how it's going, what did I say and how can we do it better.

"So a sociopath can still be a role model. They can," Larry says. "They're a role model of what not to do, which is the divine purpose. Because you have to ask yourself, 'What kind of God puts sociopaths on the planet? How can having a sociopath as a parent possibly benefit me?' And the answer is that it's the ideal role model for what not to do."

I tell Larry we become who they wanted to be, but life took over, and they followed the present day rules; it was all they knew.

"That's exactly right," Larry agrees, and we both let that thought sink in.

## Universal Insight:

*Take ownership of your shortcomings.*

# CHAPTER TWENTY THREE

## At-one-ment with My Father

*I've never seen any life transformation that didn't begin with the person in question finally getting tired of their own bullshit.*

**Elizabeth Gilbert**

Here I am now with what began the journey, the call to adventure, the monomyth of Joseph Campbell's ever-inspiring trigger that motivated me to "follow my bliss." And yes, Larry's words that he told me at our first sit-down still echo clearly in my head, "Yes, follow your bliss, but don't quit your day job." In following my own hero's journey, with the many stages from the call to adventure, refusal of the call, supernatural aid, crossing the threshold, the belly of the whale, road of trials and more – I find myself at "the atonement with the father" stage of my growing process.

Larry says, "Okay, you do understand the divine perfection of the conversation we're having today because you know what yesterday was, right? Yesterday was the Jewish holiday called Yom Kippur, the day of atonement. What atonement means if you break it down phonetically is at-one-ment. So, literally that's what the period between Rosh Hashanah and Yom Kippur is. You go through a 'clean-slate' process during the ten days between Rosh Hashanah and Yom Kippur of reviewing the year. The purpose is to take ownership of your shortcomings, ask for forgiveness and let go of them so that you're able to again be fully present with the Father and have access to all of your God-given talents and abilities for the year to come.

"Now, where NET fits in: NET is a physical process where you get to identify and eliminate the neurological entanglement of the 'sins' that you have been yet unable to let go of. What Demartini's process allows you to do is to take ownership of it. Forgive me if I sound too Catholic, Christian or whatever here, but it's only because that's where this particular concept got marketed. We are all flawed beings, and this is the process by which you take ownership of your shortcomings and be willing to let them go. Then you can access all your God-given talents and abilities, so that you have your full complement of resources to manifest what it is you're here on the planet to do I'm going to put this tongue in cheek, and I don't just mean you, Martin, I'll say 'us' because, trust me, I'm as human as the next guy. The 'overwhelm phenomena' comes about when something from the past that you're holding on to denies you access to the resources that you really have. So you feel overwhelmed.

"You see, the whole concept of a sin is the lopsided perception that because you did a particular thing, or you didn't do a certain thing, that therefore you are 'less than ....' And in the realm of being 'less than ...' comes with the perception that what you're called on to do at this moment is overwhelming. When, in fact, you are never given anything to do that's beyond your capability, except if you say so."

"That's a weight off the shoulders if you fully embrace it and apply it," I tell Larry. Larry laughs, "Well yeahhh."

He continued, "The point about that with regard to The Goodman Factor was my epiphany that that was true. I shared with you my story of jogging around the golf course at 5 a.m. when I really had a conscious sense of not being 'good enough.' And the epiphany and the language that came to me was, as near as I can tell, God saying to me, 'Dude, what do I have to do for you to know that you are a good man? Every time someone says your name it's there to remind you.' I swear to you until that particular moment in time I didn't get it. And if you'll notice I have even shifted, sometimes, for emphasis when people ask me what my name is you'll hear me say Good-man as opposed to Goodman. That's because I need to be reminded," Larry says and he starts laughing.

Now I feel divided because my last name is Casado, which translated from Spanish is "married." Larry suggests I could be married to my purpose or to my work.

I read to Larry the little blurb I have on the Atonement of the father in one of the interpretations of the 17 stages of Joseph Campbell's monomyth. I have it pasted to the back of one of my dream boards.

"In this step the person must confront and be initiated by whatever holds the ultimate power in his or her life. In many myths and stories, this is the father or a father figure who has life and death power. This is the center point of the journey."

"Yes, that is a definition of an epiphany," Larry says. 'Because in that moment of the epiphany comes the realization that there is a divine order, that there were no mistakes. If you get that there were no mistakes, forgiveness is implied because there's nothing to forgive. So if there's nothing to forgive, then there's no more 'something' in the now reminding you about your shortcomings."

That is the threshold of the atonement of where I am in my life, I tell Larry. I forgive my father, mother, all other people or situations I blame, but most importantly I forgive myself. I now embrace my "overwhelm," and I learn from it. I know now the power my father had, in his negative, unintentional way, was to teach me how to take my power back, even if he knew it or not.

## Universal Insight:

*Your ideas and thoughts are either steadied (poised)
by love or unsteadied (poisoned) by emotions.*

# CHAPTER TWENTY FOUR

# My Goodman Experience

*The meaning of life is just to be alive. It is so plain and so obvious and so simple. And yet, everybody rushes around in a great panic as if it were necessary to achieve something beyond themselves.*

**Alan Watts**

On this hero's journey, you say to yourself, "I'll show them." To only learn in this divine plan, through the trials and errors and beat down of the process, it becomes, "I only have to show myself." There's an absolute liberation behind acknowledging this source that's been with you all along. And there is no other way to learn and grow in your process if you don't hear and act on your soul's recognition to simply go and do it, do something. You just have to take action and start, whatever that may be. To do what your soul is screaming to the Universe but the clutter of your thoughts battle your dreams and rationalize you to safe, mundane values that are probably not even yours. Not all of us are cut out to do these heroic acts, and I know this because my thoughts, my upbringing and family, the friends I grew up with liked the old me. Change comes with uncertainty; it's not for the cowardly. I can only say from my own experience that separating from your old ways and crafting a new way of living won't set well with many. Those old ways will even have a convincing script to tempt you back to what was safe.

I heard Larry's mentor, Dr. John Demartini, say, "Organized knowledge is power." That statement is so powerful now in understanding where I am today. I read so much, listened to so many audio books, learned from YouTube videos about great innovators and entrepreneurs, attended seminars and courses ... I inhaled it all like a vacuum, and it became an incestuous relationship between organized knowledge and discipline. I went for my hero's journey, and it worked out, just not like anything I had planned it to be. Larry showed up in my life right when I was losing it all.

I had described myself often as being in the storm before the calm. This acquired knowledge had blown the lid off the cubicle where I once resided, the place where I blamed my environment for my actions. The truth is no one twisted my arm. I effectively created the reality I was trying to avoid. I made those decisions. As Larry often told me in my moments of impatience, "All impatience is only the result of no action." The more knowledge and understanding I developed, the more my way of life narrowed down like a funnel. In this process uprooting is inevitable, so many areas of your life will have to be released or redirected to fit through that funnel.

In my life's seven areas, for example, my family had its process. The pillars of our once family unit had fallen apart through many years of untreated hurt, which in turn separated all of us. Friends whom I valued were injecting their values into mine, and out of loyalty I submitted. I ingested bad food choices, sodas, frozen meals and weekend excesses of alcohol that not only had me gaining weight but also clouded my mind. I had no financial responsibility, weighing what I could afford versus waiting for my next paycheck. Questioning my Catholic upbringing, I combined all variations of kindness through practices I valued from Taoism to Buddhism, and more to living as a spiritual entity that aligns with one divine source or energy, call it what you may.

My eyes are wide open to the world. A guide or mentor who has a value system similar to yours, like a Larry Goodman, will teach you that, like your computer or smartphone, we also need updates to our software. They can help you understand that the update can give us a unique construction kit to help us understand our feedback loops that were set in motion long after the first time we requested them. With a little help from the Dr. Goodmans in your life, an "upgrade" to the subconscious can help you access the wisdom and the heart that can enhance your surroundings. You'll exemplify the strength, courage and resilience in becoming your authentic self and, in turn, inspire others. This is why I wrote this journey. We are not alone in this, although it sure feels that way at times.

On Wednesday nights I attend a Kundalini yoga class. The teacher, Sadhu, always gives a little pre-lecture on everyday life occurrences. He combines his narratives on a level of mental or self-awareness or even a spiritual experience with relationships or something as simple as getting mad at the Miami driver who cut you off on the way to class. On one particular day, I was considering going vegetarian or even some day going fully plant-based, but it was only a thought. That night in class when Sadhu began his lecture, and I swear to you he looked right at me, he brought up the drawbacks of animal consumption and the benefits of a vegan lifestyle. "If it's more dead than you, it's going to cost you energy at a cellular level," he said. He then looked around the class and recommended watching the movie Forks over Knives, and I was elated. Some source is talking through him and channeling me this message, amazing! How does he always know? After class, I say to the group, "Sadhu seems to always know what's on my mind and looks right at me as if that message is for me." Without missing a beat one lady says, "Oh my God, me too." Two other people add, "Yes, Sadhu is always talking about something that occurred in my life. Isn't he amazing!" I wasn't the chosen one after all, and he definitely wasn't channeling just for me. I'm still not vegan or vegetarian, yet through this understanding, I see universal consciousness at play. As much as I related it to being all about me, it's absolutely not.

"Maximum evolution occurs at the border of support and challenge," Larry echoes in my mind.

One thing Larry and I can both agree on is that this journey we have been taking together in all its 10,000 individual occurrences leads us both to each other in some divine way. It leads us to find the strength in one another that we couldn't see in ourselves. A journey that Larry had said when we first started our recordings for this book was "... about your journey, Martin's traditional process, my journey, a wise man still learning, and, in the end, it becomes the same. Our outcome is the same." We both had changed so much in the process of the two years every Friday morning at 9 a.m. sitting together, on the phone and eventually on Zoom sessions. Listen, all I knew was that The Goodman Factor worked for me and I needed to finish this book.

"From when I didn't even know a book was being written and you called me from the bookstore to tell me the working title till now, I've become both the speaker and the student on my journey," Larry says. "One of the conclusions I've come to is that's the way it's supposed to be and that, if I can surrender to the awareness that that's how it's supposed to be, it would give me the courage to keep going and dancing in the doubt of the unknown. I was raised and became a very left-brain logical, thinking, planning-oriented guy, and for most of my life I thought that was the way I was supposed to live. And so I lived that way and kept being confronted by breakdowns or limitations in that way of thinking. Each time I would be confronted by the evidence of that limitation I would conclude the reason for the conflict and the consequence was because I did something wrong. I didn't appreciate that there isn't any wrong, there isn't any right, there isn't any good, any mistake, there isn't any forward or backward. All there is the journey. It's not just my journey, it's the student's journey, it's the client's journey. Even as we're coming up with this conclusion to this book it's clear to me that the book has no actual conclusion except that it has to end somewhere. The next book will come at the next perfect time to deal with the future ideal subject."

I tell Larry, in a sense all these people who came into our lives, the alignment of mentors, they became that software update we were asking for and didn't even know that we needed it.

Larry answers, "The cycle also includes arrogance, being humbled, being made spiritually tenderized to the awareness that as long as you're a being in a body, there are going to be choices you make and consequences to those choices and opportunities to evaluate the consequences of those choices. It doesn't stop and it's never going to end. There's always going to be pain in the process. There's either going to be pain associated with continuing to drive yourself forward or the pain of the regret that comes for some people in the form of a deathbed awareness of the grief of the things they didn't do, the disappointment of that road not taken. Sometimes you don't want to play, and that's okay too. The whole point of having a tribe is the people whom I fantasized as being leaders are themselves followers as well. The people whom I perceived as having answers are living in their questions. That's the way it's supposed to be."

I asked Larry if he imagined that it would come to this when this journey started in 2015. Going through our ups and downs, switching roles at various times in the process and then getting to this completed, edited book?

Larry says, "Honestly? No. Knowing now what I know, it couldn't be any other way. The perfection of it is a little strange because there's a choice I can make at any given moment to get off the bus because the rest of the circumstances of my life have conspired to keep me engaged. Instead, the better question is why should I be exactly where I am? Why shouldn't all my finances be in perfect order? Why shouldn't I be drinking margaritas on the beach? Not that I have finite answers but I am more of a guide, sharing my vulnerability, sharing my willingness to be transparent and authentic. One of my traits is I'm a process junkie, a seeker of truth or what looked to be. As you so often have said to me on this journey, "I got this." There's nowhere else to go right now. You need to look within and trust that inner guide. That inner guide will show what it is you're here to share and the people who are ready to receive it.

"What the process is that The Goodman Factor really is all about literally is the recognition that it's all the good-man or good-woman," Larry says. "Every piece of it. It is not about letting go of anything. It's about embracing everything."

I told Larry that I needed his undivided attention as we wrapped up this finishing chapter of our lives. Recapping from our first encounter, recognition of the software updates we both encountered, our hero's journey and the completion of this book, I needed us both to take a deep breath and do a little Brendan Burchard action. Take three deep breaths and on the exhale say out loud, "Release." So Larry and I simultaneously took a deep breath and shouted "Release!" Breath in, "Release!" And one last one. Breath in, "Release!"

As our minds were fully present, I asked Larry what he wanted to conclude after this process of learning so much and even switching roles through our ups and downs in these last three years. What was his message?

Larry answered, "Everything is exactly as it should be, and the only one who hasn't seen that yet is you, the one who's living it. As long as you hold on to the notion that it's not perfect the way that it is, you give your power away and you feel powerless. We've been taught culturally to look for the power outside, when, in fact, the power is in you. I just flashed to one of my all-time favorite movies, The Wizard of Oz, and Dorothy wants to go home. All she wants to do is go home, and the good witch tells her that she had the power all along. That is my message: You have the power. You had the power all along. All you've been looking for, all you ever seek, is within you. You just need a guide to show you what you've forgotten. You already are a good man. You already are a good woman."

I am sitting with my buddy, Andres, in his studio in Miami and he's showing me some new songs he produced. He stops the music, turns to me and says, "You've grown a lot in the last three years that I've known you. This Larry guy really helped you a lot. How did he help you?" I shrugged my shoulders, folded my arms and smiled, pondering the question. After thinking about it for a little while, I replied, "You know the gasoline indicator in your car showing you if your tank is full or empty?" Andres nods his head and says "Yeah" with a confused half-smile. "Well, if you look closely at the fuel gauge you'll see a little arrow pointing either left or right, really small, next to the fuel icon. Guess what? That's to show where your gas cap is, so when you approach the gas station pumps, and you forget like I do sometimes, you know where to park your car so it's accessible to put in the fuel nozzle."

# MARTIN'S ACKNOWLEDGEMENTS

What was inspired by a title notably similar to our story (Tuesdays with Morrie by Mitch Albom) I knew I had to write this book. Recording conversation with Larry on his commute to work, I also recalled things happening in our lives when we would meet every Friday at 9 a.m. at Larry's house. I was in a transition in my life and, as fate would have it, I was lucky enough to encounter Dr. Goodman.

Before Dr. Goodman, in 2010 the The Alchemist by Paulo Coelho was the first book I heard in audio form. The effect it had sparked me to "follow my ultimate legend." That audiobook was so impactful it led me on a journey to explore every topic I wanted to learn more about and understand. That is when my inner-book nerd began in full force: Conversations with God by Neale Donald Walsch, Dr. Wayne Dyer's Living the Wisdom of the Tao, The Monk Who Sold His Ferrari by Robin Sharma, Peaks and Valleys by Spencer Johnson, Power vs. Force by David R. Hawkins, M.D., Ph.D., Think and Grow Rich by Napoleon Hill, The Icarus Deception by Seth Godin, The Go-Giver by Bob Burg and John D. Mann. Then the real physical books came after.

I was obsessed and unlearning to re-learn. One of my all-time favorites was the audio on The Power of Myth by Joseph Campbell. He rocked my core to the point of leaving my family company in 2013 on my own hero's journey. Of course, Tony Robbins on my CDs when I was 19 echoes in my mind saying "Take ultimate action" in his raspy voice.

Thank you to my most recent influencers, in no particular order like Brendon Burchard, Dr. John Demartini, Joe Dispenza, Tim Ferriss, Lewis Howes, Paul Chek, Yo Elliott-Elliott Hulse, Brian Rose of London Real, the motivating Gary Vaynerchuk, Grant Cardone on sales, The MFCEO Project's Andy Frisella and so many more. I'm forever grateful for your stories and triumphs amongst the animosity. Thank you for sharing your struggle to strive.

Thank you, Dr. Goodman, for being my mentor, supervisor and ultimately a best friend through this journey. Lastly, thank you, Dad, for this drive I have because of your iron-clad fist of loving strict discipline. I love you.

# ABOUT MARTIN CASADO

My father came to the United States from Chile and met my American/Hispanic mother in Miami, Florida, where I was born and raised. My parents have been divorced now for many years. I have two siblings, a younger sister and younger brother. Since I was 11, all I knew was working my father's logistics company sweeping the floor to being the warehouse manager. The predicament was that I loved, and I was good at, drawing, graphic design and songwriting with my guitar but I didn't know how to pursue these urges. I was able to do work on some of my passion projects after hours, and I wrote the songs and produced two albums, one in Spanish (which we produced in Quito, Ecuador) and one in English (produced in Miami, Florida). In a successful family company and being the oldest son, I felt an obligation to take the reins. I quit the first time in 2006 and worked for an ad agency while getting a bachelor's degree in graphic design. Two years later I left the ad agency and started my own design company called Nitram Communication + Design. Then, I was asked to come back to the family business by my father in 2010, and out of loyalty I did. In this time I acquired a voracious appetite for audiobooks during my commute to work, reading every day, YouTube videos, online courses and mentors. In 2013, I had to take a stance on my own life's callings to follow my bliss and I resigned. Two years later, overloaded with knowledge and little wisdom about my next direction in life, losing it all, the teacher appeared and I met Dr. Larry Goodman.

As a former client, this book is a testimonial to Dr. Goodman. His one-on-one personal coaching changed my life in so many ways. At times, our roles reversed, and I helped him. Years later I am still mentored by Dr. Goodman. A friendship established and we started to work together and combine our strengths to deliver The Goodman Factor. We've worked long and hard finding our part and experience in human behavior and changes in our own lives to help ourselves, and in turn, we hope to inspire and help others.

# LARRY'S ACKNOWLEDGEMENTS

Having a virtually photographic memory has drawbacks and benefits. The benefits are I am never at a loss for material. The disadvantages are I don't always remember them exactly verbatim, and after 63 years I can't tell you where some of this stuff comes from anymore. We've done an exhaustive job trying to cite sources with full acknowledgment. That is and was our intention. The purpose of this book is to share with others what was life changing for us in the hope that it will add value to the reader, or at least be entertaining. The universe rewards action. So if you are reading something here that speaks to you, do something about it or with it.

I want to personally thank my parents, my wife Sally, my daughter Alexa and a list of mentors and teachers from Drs. Deb and Scott Walker, Dr. John Demartini, Dr. Josh Wagner, Dr. Nima Rhamany, Dr. Maggie Mauer - my NET buddy, and a list of mentors too long to list here.

And most of all, I'd like to thank Martin Casado, without whose persistence and perseverance and belief in me and my hero's journey, this book would not exist or at least would not have been finished and brought to share with all of you.

# ABOUT DR. LARRY GOODMAN

My name is Dr. Larry Goodman, and before I began to study the universal laws of success, health and happiness, I was just like you.

In the early 90s, I was dealing with a series of events that would change my life forever. I felt lost. I didn't know what to do. So, one day I decided that I needed to educate myself. I began traveling all over the world to seek out the best healers, researchers and teachers to see if they could help me solve my problems. It was a difficult journey to begin and even more difficult to complete, but I knew that if I didn't put in the work and make sacrifices, I would never achieve happiness.

Since attending my first Breakthrough Experience in 1992 and first NET (neuro emotional technique) seminar that same year, I have been studying, researching, writing and teaching in the areas of human behavior, success and mind/body healing and stress.

This has led me to acquire advanced training, certifications and skills in many areas. I contribute programs and protocols in NET as well as complete training and presentation of programs for continuing education in chiropractic for state and national organizations as well as chiropractic colleges and medical schools.

My drive for The Goodman Factor finds the blocks we tell our own belief systems. I help you reconnect to your purpose in both business and in personal lives. My various techniques and experience will take you from stuck to full awareness of your own personal being.

# DOWNLOAD OUR FREE ASSESMENT WHEEL (AGAIN) AND SEE HOW YOUR LIFE HAS GOTTEN GOODER!

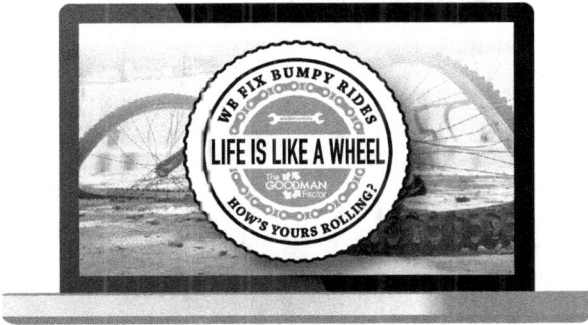

To say thank you AGAIN. We've created this tool to allow you to visually determine how your life is rolling and why? We would like to give you the wheel for FREE.

Even if you're thinking you know why your life STILL sucks we've create this tool to help you gain awareness and perspective. If you want to go from GOODER TO YOUR GOODEST LIFE check out our video, link below.

## DON'T WAIT!

**Watch a FREE VIDEO TRAINING today and hope to see you at the next level of YOUR GOODEST LIFE:**

www.goodmanfactor.com/lifeislikeawheel

# YOUR GOODEST LIFE!

*LOADING...*

www.ingramcontent.com/pod-product-compliance
Lightning Source LLC
LaVergne TN
LVHW050045090426
835510LV00043B/3025